I0393445

Making eBooks
How To Make and Publish your Books With Free Tools

by Michael Lynnmore

Table of Contents

Copyright

Introduction

What if you could control the entire process of writing your book, production and distribution using free tools? You can. This book shows you how to do that. This book assumes you have a computer and access to the internet.

Sure, you can pay other people to convert your content into an eBook for you, each time you need a conversion. If that's your plan, you do not need this book. If you'd rather easily do it yourself for free, as many times as you'd like, then this book is for you.

 You don't need to get this book to figure this out. You can figure it out for yourself if you'd like. This book simply helps people learn from what I learned while I figured it out.

Making eBooks is still a process in its infancy as our society transitions from paper publishing to electronic publishing. Nicolas Negroponte discussed the differences between bits and atoms in his 1995 book *Being Digital*. Twenty one years later, we're just starting to achieve momentum with digital publishing as more eBooks are sold than paper books. Atoms make up the physical objects in our world such as plastic DVDs, CDs, and paper books. Digital information, like eBooks, are made up of bits, the smallest unit of information on a computer. The tools have advanced for publishing digital or electronic books, sometimes called eBooks.

The process is sure to change as tools continue to improve.

Creating this book was fun. Just making the book made it a successful project for me. I enjoyed making it. Perhaps you will enjoy making your own eBooks and print books this way too.

The journey to discover how and **the challenge** of getting it right **drew me in**. After much trial and error, when **I finally got it all working** I felt like jumping in the air and shouting Eureka!

This book also **extends my own memory** of how I made and published eBooks and print books. I wrote this book because if life takes me on a different path for too long and I forget how I did it, then this book is my own "how to" instructions **to my future self** when I need to write and publish again. Potentially other people may see the value of this book too.

One last point. There exist some excellent online tools that I don't show in this book because I don't want them to disappear during a project if they run out of startup money and go out of business. The tools I chose to use and explain in this book are downloadable. This lets you have control of your project's infrastructure. You may want to use those online tools. I'm only showing how to use the ones you can download.

Preface

There is much free information on the internet about how to use plain text AsciiDoc and apps like AsciiDoctor to render it to other formats like PDF, HTML, and eBooks. Much of free information on the internet about AsciiDoctor was written by Dan Allen and I am grateful for his efforts. You are welcome to use these other materials. This book represents my learning from these sources and stumbling to solutions for things.

Many sites in the community presume you are a software developer. This means they sometimes inadvertently leave out much how-to information because they presume that software developers already know how to do the particular task.

My audience is writers who are not software developers. This includes nonfiction writers and technical writers. They may have some exposure to software concepts and practices, but if not I will walk them through the step-by-step actions needed so they don't have to stumble around to learn as I did.

Let me know if I accidentally did the same thing to you. If there are erroneous assumptions, please let me know and I'll fix them.

Acknowledgements

Thank you to the creator of AsciiDoc, Stuart Rackham, and to the community of AsciiDoc users that are so helpful with their comments and postings.

Also thanks to Dan Allen, the creator of AsciiDoctor, for trying to solve the question, *"What if you could write books like you write e-mail?"* Dan did a great job making the app and describing it to the world. Dan also focuses his writing and remarks to an audience that is experienced in software development. This book tries to also address the needs of people without a software development background. These gaps were the impetus for this book.

I have found it easier to use AsciiDoctor to render AsciiDoc files into various formats than other options.

And I'd also like to thank Hubert Klein Ikkink, perhaps known better as mrhaki.

AsciiDoctor builds on the creations of Norm Walsh with his DocBook work. Thanks Norm for your XML specification for making books and the XSLT tools to render the XML to PDFs, HTML, and eBooks.

And lastly, to the creators of the Google search engine, without which I'd have to work so much harder.

Conventions Used

The following conventions are used:

For showing exactly what should be typed into the command line, a different font will be used as in the following example.

```
cd mydirectory
```

The following admonitions will be used to draw your attention.

Notes are used to highlight important information or to present asides relevant to the topic at hand.

Tips provide helpful information on how to most effectively use a particular idea.

Warnings alert you to significant difficulties that may occur.

Cautions alert you to potential difficulties that may occur.

I will also show examples of AsciiDoc plain text. These examples will be formatted as plain text like the following example, sometimes including callouts that I use to describe a specific spot in the AsciiDoc plain text:

```
== My Chapter Title  ①
My first paragraph is here.
This is just an example paragraph, so there is nothing
exciting about it.

My next paragraph is separated by a blank line to let the
rendering app know that this is a new paragraph.  ②
So I can include other information in this paragraph that
will be separate from the preceding paragraph.

=== My Section Title Goes Here  ③
Here is another example paragraph.
Blah blah blah.
```

① The chapter title only has two equal signs in front of the title.

② A blank line separates the paragraphs.

③ The section title has three equals signs in front of the title.

Why Use Plain Text

This chapter describes why I use plain text for book projects and why I think you should consider it too.

This chapter tells you **why** I do it.

Why Not Microsoft Word

My family prefers using Microsoft Word. They asked me, *"Why would you want to use anything other than Word?"*

Given the proliferation of authoring tools available in mobile authoring applications (apps), cloud service authoring apps and PC authoring apps, there are many choices today. Each of us has our own preferences for tools. There's no requirement for you to change. I'm just describing why I use a mature, **FREE** plain-text writing format. You may decide you like it too.

Commercial Tools have Restrictions

Commercial tools, like Microsoft Word, often:

- Make it easy to start and difficult to finish (publish)
- Cost money to license and use legally
- Have licensing models that are increasingly moving from perpetual licenses (buy once and use forever) to subscription models (pay monthly)
- Use restricted proprietary data formats to store your content, often binary formats, that are unsuitable for long-lasting information

- Change to new versions that are sometimes not backwards compatible to the older version

- Controlled by private companies that can change their tool at their whim

- May not work easily across many devices and operating systems (Windows, MacOS, Linux)

- Can be shut down without releasing the app to open source if their tool was not as economically rewarding as expected

- Can be difficult to convert to other formats

- May not support a modular writing approach

- Break and stop working when you use large documents. Nonfiction books range from 40,000–50,000 words for a medium-sized book to 60,000–70,000 words for a long nonfiction book.

Plain Text is Free

Here are some of the reasons I like plain text.

- **Plain text is free.** [1: Plain text is free if you already have a computer.]

- **There are no costs to get plain text.** [2: You will need internet access to download the tools in this book.]

- There are no licensing monthly or annual fees for plain text.

- Plain text does not belong to anyone, except you the copyright holder of your own ideas.

- There are many free tools to use plain text. Of course you can also pay for commercial tools, if you want to.

Plain Text Lasts Decades

Here's why I don't use Microsoft Word to write long books. I'm old enough to have seen PC word processing apps, like Microsoft Word, change over the years and not be backwards compatible to prior versions. I watched the Word Perfect word processor app disappear from the market. I've had the pain of spending hours converting large and older content formats from a few years ago to the latest version. I now prefer a format for my long written work that lasts for 10 to 20 years or more. I occasionally use word processing apps for short documents.

The only *easy* format that I have discovered lasts decades, so far, is plain text.

I use plain text now for writing books, backup files and archived versions, confident that I can easily use my writing again in ten years if needed.

The reason I qualified with the word *easy*, is that for a while when I worked in technical writing professionally The technical communications industry focused on extensible markup language (XML). If you have never been involved in technical writing, and never plan to, you may want to skip the rest of this paragraph. I have used SGML, DocBook XML, DITA XML, S1000D XML and other MIL standard XML specifications for the government. These format specifications last a long time as well. But even people in the technical communications industry know that these complicated formats change over time with different versions. Another challenge with XML is having to find commercial authoring applications that validate the XML to a DTD or schema. When writing for myself, I don't want to have to pay for all those tools. Additionally, XML can be a challenging source format to read because of all the verbose markup.

Then along came markdown. I investigated markdown and liked it for simple documents like blog entries or uncomplicated documents. But I became frustrated anytime I wrote a complicated document, because markdown couldn't handle it. That I discovered an older plain text format called AsciiDoc That was created to get around the difficulties of using DocBook XML. It's a lot like markdown, it handles complex documents, and the tools are free.

> The single biggest source of inspiration for Markdown's syntax is the format of plain text e-mail.
>
> — John Gruber, Creator of Markdown

What Does ASCII Even Mean?

My teen son asked me one day, "What does ascii mean?" I told him that when computers started in the United States that their creators used the English alphabet and Arabic numerals. The set of characters was called ASCII. I remembered it stood for something, but I had to look it up to remember it stood for the American Standard Code for Information Interchange (ASCII). Later, as computers spread across the globe, a more extensive set of characters called Unicode was developed To include characters used in all languages of the world. That was about all the information about ASCII my son cared about. I'm guessing that's enough to satisfy your curiosity too.

Plain Text Lets Us Write Once, Publish Everywhere

Call me lazy, but I only want to write my content once. I like formats, like plain text, that allow me to publish to Adobe PDF, EPUB for e-readers, Amazons format for Kindle readers and to HTML5 for web formats without having to recreate the content for each format. So part of my criteria for a great set of book making tools, is the capability to easily publish to all formats with the least manual effort possible. I like automation.

Now, I can hear some of you current Microsoft Word users saying that Word already allows me to publish to PDF, HTML and to print. You're correct, many authoring apps now offer the functionality of publishing to many formats. However, see the prior section on the authoring format lasting decades.

Plain Text Means Authoring Before Formatting

I prefer a writing process that's uncluttered, with minimal distractions and interruptions. In other words, I prefer a writing process where I think about what to write. William Zensner said that it takes **clear thinking** to have **clear writing**. [3: See the book *On Writing Well*, by William Zensner] If the authoring app forces me to deal with fonts, styles, and layout issues, it distracts me from my thinking and interrupts the writing process. After years of working with offering applications that offer *what you see is what you get* (WYSIWYG), I have decided to do the writing first, and the formatting second in multiple iterations rather than trying to do everything at once. This idea of separating content from display formatting can make you more productive.

Some people even advocate for authoring directly in HTML. I've done this and it is distracting during the authoring process. I don't recommend it because it is another example of mixing the writing process and the formatting process.

Some authoring apps are now offering features that minimize distractions and interruptions. That's good.

Plain Text Allows Sharing With Others—Non-Proprietary Formats

Another reason I prefer plain text format is that I can share it easily with other people. [4: I shared a genealogy book I wrote with AsciiDoc with my father.]

They don't have to buy the same software authoring application that I use to create it, so they can read it. This can be helpful when you're asking reviewers to review your work, although I send reviewers a published format like PDF, or HTML. I don't like my writing being locked up in some company's proprietary format.

Plain Text Lets Us Write Using Many Devices

In my Granddad's day, he wrote mostly on a manual typewriter. His *mobile app* was pen and paper. At one point I only wrote with a Windows PC. Then I got a linux machine. Nothing on my linux machines worked like it did on the Windows PC. Then I got a Mac. The Mac worked similar to a linux machine, but still not like a Windows PC. Now, I also use mobile devices for authoring apps, because they're convenient to convert otherwise dead time into productive writing time. But Apple's restrictions on file access means that plain text also helps get my content out of the mobile device and into another system.

I've experienced the frustrations of trying to move my writing across platforms (Windows, Linux, Mac OS, iOS). For me, one of the best aspects of using plain text to write is that plain text files transfer across platforms easily using **dropbox** or some other cloud-based storage service.

Plain Text Offers Easy Conversion to Other Formats

Plain text can be converted into any other format with no loss of information. Specific markdown formats may require special conversion tools. [5: See Pandoc as a free and nearly universal conversion tool]

Plain Text Offers Modular Writing as an Option

We don't always create of a book in the order the readers see it after its published. Sometimes a flash of insight comes for topic D rather than in a linear way of A, then B, then C, then D.

I build my nonfiction books by starting with a mind map of the content. [6: See Using a Free mind mapping Tool to Design your Book for more detail.] This helps me determine what goes in the book's scope and what does not. So I may write a section or chapter about topic D first.

Some people prefer to write their entire book in one big **monolithic** file. AsciiDoc allows writing everything in one great big file as one way to build a book. This can make things easier for global find/replace during editing and reviews.

I prefer tools that allow me to write in a **modular way**. AsciiDoc allows modular building of book content as another option. Modular writing works well for teams of writers collaborating too.

Some people prefer the granularity of chapters to build up the book. I prefer sections or topics as the granularity that's "just right" for me. Not too big, and not too small of modular chunks.

This means I build the book with my **lego-like blocks of separate writing files**. Sometimes I change my mind and move things around. If my authoring tool set allows me to easily move the order of these files, I'm happy. So when we buy Legos and use the instructions (**like a map** of where to put the blocks) to put the blocks in the right places, we end up with the intended Lego toy at the end of the process.

Modular chunks impacts editing and review a little bit, in that you have to note the section the change is in so you can find the file that chunk of content is in.

> SIDEBAR: I record the phrase I'm looking for and search for the phrase in a rendered version of the book draft, say the HTML file. This lets me find that content quickly. Then I can back up to the parent heading of the section or topic of that phrase. And finally, I find the file that matches the heading so I can make the edit. This may sound hard, but the advantage is that when actually editing my modular chunks, I'm working with smaller files that makes it easier to navigate to the place to fix.

This modular approach lets me focus on smaller chunks of the book at a time.

Nonfiction books often includes glossary entries. I can reuse my glossary entries in other books without having to copy and paste them in.

I like when the tool allows me to create a *map* of sorts that tells the tool how to build the content from my lego blocks of plain text files. When the tool is done, I get my book in the order I specified in my map. [7: I grew to appreciate this way of modular writing while using DITA XML and S1000D XML.]

> If you write in Microsoft Word, it's easy to get stuck in a linear way of thinking. It's not easy to back track and find that one spot where that one scene happened that's now relevant four chapters later. All that scrolling.
>
> The danger of writing with Microsoft Word—or any program that doesn't allow you to organize your chapters and scenes or sections as you would keep a physical binder—is that your writing process changes to reflect your writing tools.
>
> — Amanda Shofner

Plain Text Lets Us Fix the Styling in One Place and Have it Apply Globally

Rather than having to go back through the entire manuscript at the end and make changes in every location, I can update the style sheet and have the change flow to every instance throughout the entire manuscript. [8: Not being able to apply style globally is my main issue with the Scrivener app because it encodes the content in Rich Text Format (RTF). Although you can adjust the app to use multi markdown. Otherwise, I like the

Plain Text Lets Us Use Free Versioning Tools

I like plain text too because I can take advantage of versioning tools originally built for software developers that also work when I write in plain text.

One of the benefits of this is seeing differences between versions. I use a convention of one sentence per line in the source plain text file. The tool that renders my plain text to formatted PDF, eBook, or HTML combines these into paragraphs like normal.

Then I get to see what changed sentence by sentence. It also makes it easier to see when I have a sentence that is too long.

My Journey to AsciiDoc for Plain Text Writing

I first looked into AsciiDoc after my frustrations with markdown. I got excited about how easy markdown was compared to XML. I had a new computer and did not want to buy expensive validating editors for XML again. Markdown looked like a great solution so I started using it. Markdown worked great for my simple documents. But I had already experienced the full power of XML for documentation and markdown began to breakdown for me in more complex documentation situations. I still like markdown for uncomplicated writing.

My curiosity took me down the AsciiDoc path after markdown was found wanting. I found that AsciiDoc works. I stumbled with the setup. That part was a bit challenging. Then when writing with AsciiDoc, I hit the repeated *"How do I do this or that?"* questions and looking it up with Google's search engine.

Then like a child learning to hold and write with a pencil or pen, my ability grew to where I could express myself with AsciiDoc with less and less syntax lookups and more and more focus on my thinking so I could have clear writing.

This book is the result of my learning to wield AsciiDoc quickly to make books with **free** tools.

The Next Best Thing—Scrivener

If I'm unsuccessful convincing you to use plain text free tools, then I'd recommend the inexpensive Scrivener (I paid $45 USD) app as the next best thing. [9: See the Scrivener site at https://www.literatureandlatte.com] It does many of the same things with a familiar graphical user interface. I have it on my Mac, PC, and iPad.

Why Do-It-Yourself (DIY)

Now that I've covered why I use plain text, this chapter tells you **how** I do it. It describes why I publish my own books rather than use traditional publishers.

Some of us in the United States go to Home Depot or Lowes to get supplies to perform do-it-yourself projects around our houses. I do it because it can be less expensive than hiring out all the work and I enjoy some types of DIY work.

This book shows a similar pattern of a do-it-yourself project for self-publishing, and for pushing a book out to various formats using free tools. It costs you no money for the free tools. It will cost a little bit of time to install them. I show you how to use the free tools. Once you've got the habits down, **self publishing is very fast and very easy with these tools**. You may want to write and self publish more than one book, so these methods will help you each time you write a new book.

After the non-recurring setup work it only takes seconds for me to publish to HTML and a couple of minutes to publish to PDF for print.

 My first time took me longer. Your first time will likely take you longer too. But as you make less mistakes, it speeds up and you can produce a book very quickly.

If you're a writer, you still have to write. Authoring the content is not automated. Even if you use a traditional publisher, you still have to do the hard work of writing the book.

Publishers will do the work of publishing to eBooks and print books for your, but at great cost in time, control, and less payment per copy purchased.

Just like a DIY project at your house, the first time you have to replace an insect screen on your door it can seem tedious, slow and frustrating as you learn what you're doing.

Likewise for your book, using plain text tools the first time through will seem tedious, slow and frustrating as you learn what you're doing.

Today I can put a new insect screen on pretty quickly. [10: Our dogs provide multiple opportunities to replace insect screens as they occasionally shred the screens.] I can also publish my books in minutes. Literally. I've timed it.

The same thing that drives me to do DIY in other areas pushes me to try DIY for book publishing too.

Why I like DIY Projects for Making Books

- DIY helps me lean towards a growth mindset. [11: See the book *Mindset: The New Psychology of Success,* by Carol Dweck for more details.]

- I get to make something, and I like creating.

- Mastering something I'm interested in is satisfying, even when it takes work.

- I get to learn from my mistakes and improve.

- It will be much easier the second time around.

- I build confidence in these regularly used skills.

- I get hands-on so I can help move towards my goals or even dreams.

- I gain new skills or knowledge. Each book project I take on teaches me something new and improves my problem-solving abilities. I get to use my brain more.

- Freedom. DIY offers me more autonomy than traditional publishing where you yield to the publisher's processes and conventions.

 If you're the type of person who can't stand spending more than five minutes learning something new, then this book is probably not for you. If you like DIY projects, keep going and I'll walk you through it.

I like books. So I apply DIY for myself and share with you. I don't enjoy plumbing. So, I hire out toilet fixes.

Time shifting occurs too. For example, when you first buy Microsoft Word and install it, you have to learn how to use the app. Learning to use Microsoft Word for the basics is not too difficult up-front. However, the little time spent up front is dwarfed by the time spent near the end of your project trying to get Microsoft Word to publish a 400-page book. At the end, you'll run into many problems with Microsoft Word. If you end up with a corrupted file like I have, you'll really be in a pickle.

Consider where you'll spend your time. AsciiDoc moves the effort to the front, where Microsoft Word makes you spend that time at the end of your project. AsciiDoc does not take much at the end to publish. But you have to learn how to use it up front. Making some words bold is the same in both apps. The hurdle at the front rather than at the back is what throws some people off. However, the publishing savings with AsciiDoc ends up saving time overall as compared to Microsoft Word and other word processing apps.

This book took 1 second to render to HTML. It took 46 seconds to render to a PDF. This final book is over 18,000 words.

I've created many other books, some over 650 pages, and they all take a similarly short time to produce for publication or distribution.

In summary, now you know **how** I do it. I use the do-it-yourself approach.

The remainder of this book will show you **what** I do so you can do it too.

If when you follow these instructions your results don't work, it is easy to get frustrated. I got frustrated when learning and my results did not match the instructions written to software developers. Methodically go through the error messages and work your way to the mistake so you can correct it and move on. See my lessons learned in Gotchas. When we're new to something we introduce errors unintentionally. I did. You likely will. Don't quit. Talk a walk. Get a good night's sleep and try again when you're fresh. The most difficult part is the setup of tools. Fortunately, you only have to do this once per computer you buy. [13: If you choose to update the tools, you'll have to update them occasionally.]

By Example

For me, I've always learned best from books that show examples. In particular, I appreciate when the examples are consistent throughout and used to illustrate each new thing I'm learning so I can check my understanding as I go against the worked example that the author provided.

So I will use some examples from this book, and other examples that are shorter. Initially I used some empty text or fake text called lorem ipsum text too.

So for example, here is this section written in AsciiDoc plain text format:

```
== By Example ①
For me, I've always learned best from books that show
examples. ②
In particular, I appreciate when the examples are
consistent throughout and used to illustrate each new
thing I'm learning so I can check my understanding as I
go.
        ③
So I decided to use examples from this book in most
cases. ④
Initially I used some empty text or fake text called
lorem ipsum text too.

So for example, here is this section written in AsciiDoc
plain text format: ⑤
```

① The "== " indicates a title.

② First paragraph

③ Paragraph break

④ Second paragraph

⑤ Third paragraph

This example shows how easy plain text is to write. There is very little markup. I'll show more specifics as we go in the book.

Then by using these examples, you can build your AsciiDoc skills a layer at a time. This follows the pattern of building skill with gradually building challenge. As you build the skill, then you will see productivity gains like I've experienced.

Non-Recurring Set Up for Authoring

It may seem hard to install tools, but it is worth it later in saved time. We'll start with only the tools to create content. You will need the following apps:

- Internet Browser
- Text Editor

Internet Browser

Your computer should come with an internet browser, but if not then install Chrome or Firefox. You will need this to see the HTML versions of your book.

Installing the Atom Text Editor

You can use any text editor you'd like to author your book content. Many people use TextMate on Mac. I'm going to show Atom because it is cross platform.

Installing Atom can go smoothly.

1. Go to https://atom.io.
2. Look on the page for a download button.

 The button or buttons should be specific to your platform and the download package should be easily installable if you have administrator privileges on your computer.

This section only discusses how to install the authoring tools. To install the publishing tools, I cover that in Non-Recurring Setup - Rendering AsciiDoc to Other Formats.

Fast Prototyping

Before we go straight to writing, I want to show you a tool to help write to your audience more quickly. First, let's define what I mean by prototyping.

prototyping

Prototyping for books is the activity of creating a table of contents or an incomplete version of the book being authored. Think of a prototype as a draft version of your book that allows you to explore your ideas and show the intention behind your content structure or the overall design concept to potential audience members before investing time and money in authoring content the audience may not value. It is much cheaper to change a book early in the authoring process than to make changes after you write the book. So, consider building prototypes early in the process. Prototyping allows you to gather feedback from potential audience members while you are still planning and designing your book's content.

Free tools allow you to prototype and fail fast as you search for customers. Free tools can also make your experiments smaller in impact, learning about what audiences value and will pay for with little to no costs.

I use mindmaps to prototype books. I'll define a mindmap as:

mindmap

A mind map is a diagram used to visually organize information. A mind map is hierarchical and shows relationships among pieces of the whole. It is often created around a single concept, drawn as an image in the center of a blank page, to which associated representations of ideas such as images, words and parts of words are added. Major ideas are connected directly to the central concept, and other ideas branch out from those. [14: Definition from Wikipedia at https://en.wikipedia.org/wiki/Mind_map.]

Mind maps also have the benefit of helping create a fast prototype of your book for getting feedback. Here is the process I use for nonfiction books.

1. Create your book structure in your mind map.

2. Include the major topics (chapters) and their children (sections or topics).

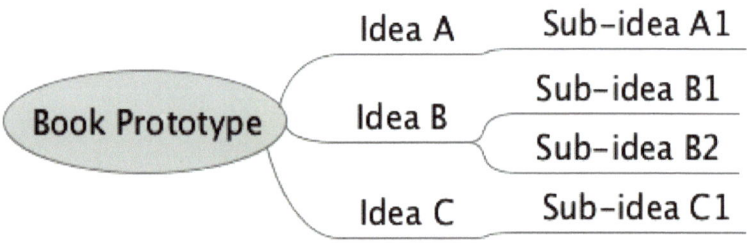

Figure 1. Prototype Mind Map Example

3. Make an empty book prototype *.adoc plain text file.

4. Add your book title and author attributes.

```
= AsciiDoc Authoring: How To Make Books For Free ①
:author: Michael Lynnmore ②
```

① Book title and optionally a subtitle after a colon

② Author attribute and author name. Note there are no empty lines between the title line and the attribute lines below it.

5. Copy the map's central node, for example "Book Prototype", and paste into your empty AsciiDoc book text file. It will all

the sub branches and copy them too as shown in the following example.

```
= AsciiDoc Authoring: How To Make Books For Free
:author: Michael Lynnmore

Book Prototype ①
    Idea A ②
        Sub-idea A1 ③
    Idea B
        Sub-idea B1
        Sub-idea B2
    Idea C
        Sub-idea C1
```

① Remove the mind map title

② Replace single tab with two equal signs

③ Replace two tabs with three equal signs

6. Note how the Freemind paste of the map indents the child nodes nicely so you can see the hierarchy from the mind map.

7. Change the indents to the correct number of equal signs so AsciiDoctor can assign the right title hierarchy.

8. Now add a table of contents attribute.

```
= AsciiDoc Authoring: How To Make Books For Free
:author: Michael Lynnmore
:toc: top
:toclevels: 2

== Idea A

=== Sub-idea A1

== Idea B

=== Sub-idea B1

=== Sub-idea B2

== Idea C

=== Sub-idea C1
```

9. Use AsciiDoctor to render the prototype file to HTML or PDF.

   a. Use the rendering **instructions in another part of this book.**

   b. My prototype folder looks like this when done.

Figure 2. Prototype Files in my Folder

10. Show the result to a potential member of your intended audience for some feedback.

   a. Point out the title page.

   b. Point out the table of contents.

c. Tell them that the book has not been written yet, so you'd appreciate their feedback on the scope of the contents just based on the table of contents.

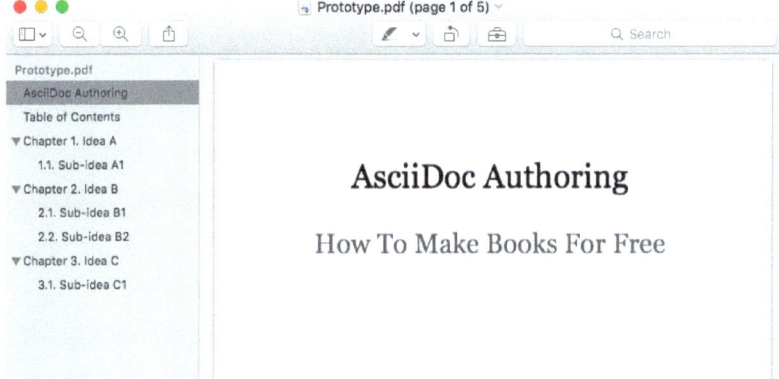

Figure 3. Prototype First Page

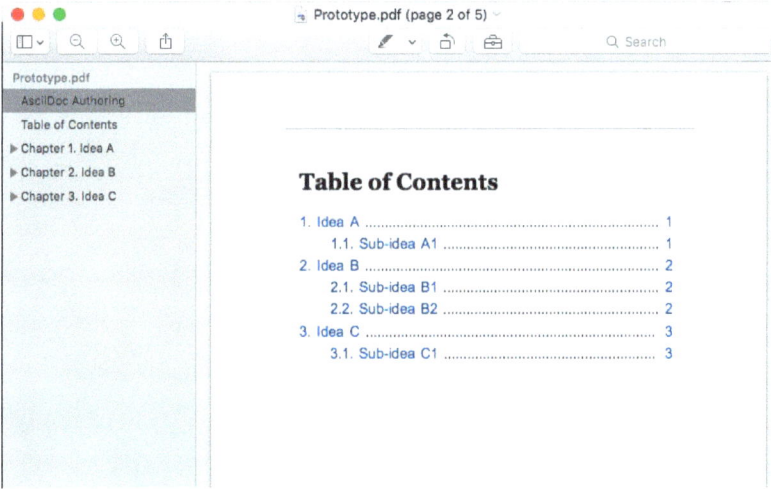

Figure 4. Prototype TOC Page

The **free** mindmapping/prototyping tool I use I'll describe in the next section.

Using a Free mind mapping Tool to Design your Book

I have found mind maps to be a fast way to build up ideas. The best free mind mapping app I have found is a cross platform app called Freemind.

Freemind is an nicely made free app to make mind maps on computers (Mac, Windows, and Linux). You can also draw a mind map on a piece of paper with a pencil or pen. I prefer mind map apps because I can easily move things around while designing the structure of the book.

To install it, follow these instructions.

1. Go to http://freemind.sourceforge.net/wiki/index.php/Download.

2. Select the download for your platform.

3. Follow instructions on their site.

4. Open the Freemind app.

5. Use the menus **File | New** to create a new map.

6. Start with your main project.

7. Add branches to map out your ideas for the scope of your book.

8. Save the mind map to your project folder. The filename extension is *.mm

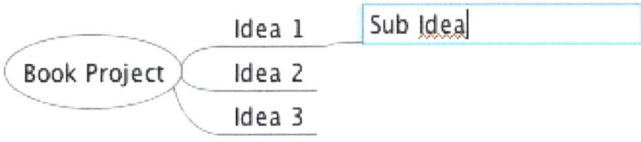

Figure 5. Example mind map Using Freemind

The benefits of mind mapping include:

- The mind mapping method is **simple to use**
- mind mapping is **non-linear**, the way my brain works when creating, flitting from idea to idea
- mind maps are **visual**, showing the relationships among the ideas helping me get my thinking clear before writing
- I can quickly prototype a book without any setup time for the authoring tools
- mind mapping increases my creativity because I can **see the associative relationships** as I build it out
- mind mapping increases my productivity because it lets me **generate more ideas quickly** and sort out my thoughts with a few words or phrases per branch
- If you're collaborating, a mind map helps get **everyone's thoughts on the same page**

For more information about how to mind map, see *The Mind Map Book: How to Use Radiant Thinking to Maximize Your Brain's Untapped Potential*, by Tony Buzan.

There are good paid apps for mind mapping too, but this book is about the free tools. I have used Freemind to mind map for over 15 years and it works great. Mind mapping works wonderfully for me.

Using the Command Line or Terminal

Many people have never used the command line (Windows) or terminal (Mac) before. So let's walk through step-by-step how to use the command line, which you will use for plain text authoring with AsciiDoc. You will **see how easy it is to use** when someone shows you how.

 If you already know how to use the terminal or command line, you can skip this chapter.

On a Mac

The command line on a Mac is called the terminal.

1. On MacOS, open launchpad.

Figure 6. Using Launchpad

2. In the search bar at the top of the screen, type **terminal** and the terminal icon appears.

34

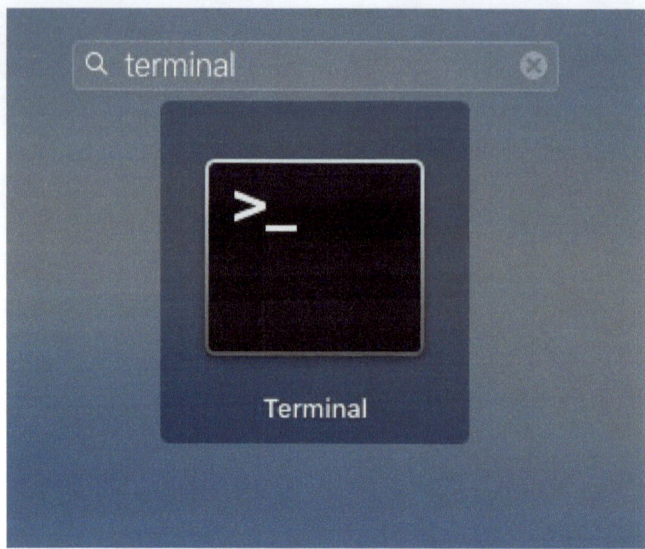

Figure 7. Terminal Icon

3. Select the terminal icon.

4. See the black terminal window appear.

Figure 8. Terminal Window

Another method on the Mac is to open your Applications folder, then open the Utilities folder, and then open the Terminal application.

You will use the terminal enough to want to dock it on your Mac dock bar.

Figure 9. Dock the Terminal

On a Windows PC

1. Click Start.

2. In the Search bar or Run line type **cmd** and press enter.

3. See the black window command line window appear.

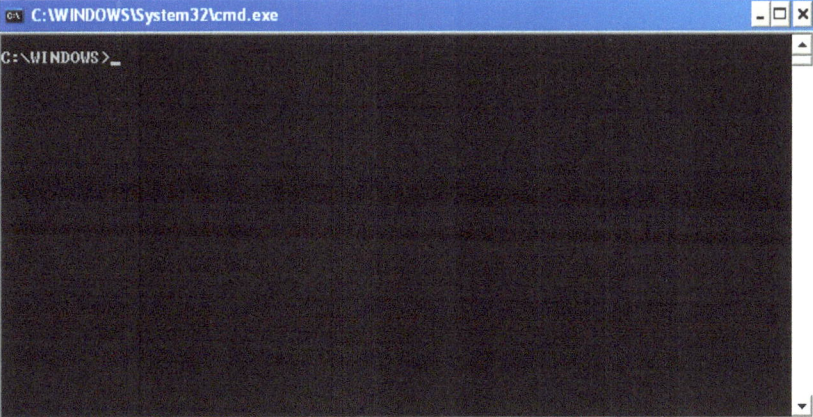

Figure 10. Windows Command Line

Your First AsciiDoc Book Attempt/Iteration

The first time you try anything new, it can seem hard or even intimidating. The first time you try AsciiDoc is no different. AsciiDoc is easy to use, so let's walk through it step-by-step.

If you have never used the terminal or command line, see Using the Command Line or Terminal before starting this chapter.

Work Area

First, let's set up a working area on our computer. You only need to do this setup once per book project.

I called my folder *AsciiDoc_Book* because it is for this book. Name your folder a name that you'll recognize for your own book.

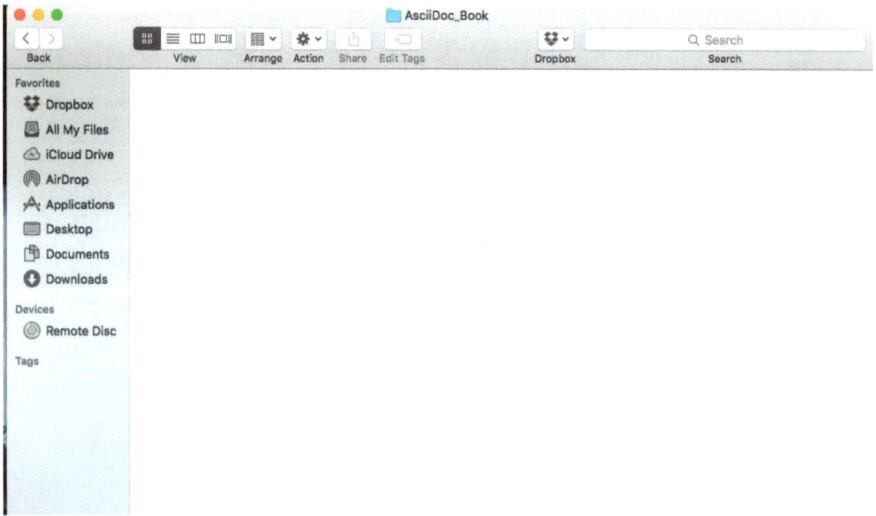

Figure 11. Make an Empty Folder

Next, let's set up the work area with some folders to organize things.

On a Mac, you can left click and select **New Folder** or use the terminal to make new folders.

Make a folder for the following:

- Media (images, video, audio files)

- Chapters and Sections (or you can call this topics)

- eBook

- PrintPDF

- Optionally, add a folder for glossary terms if you plan to include a big glossary and would like to reuse terms.

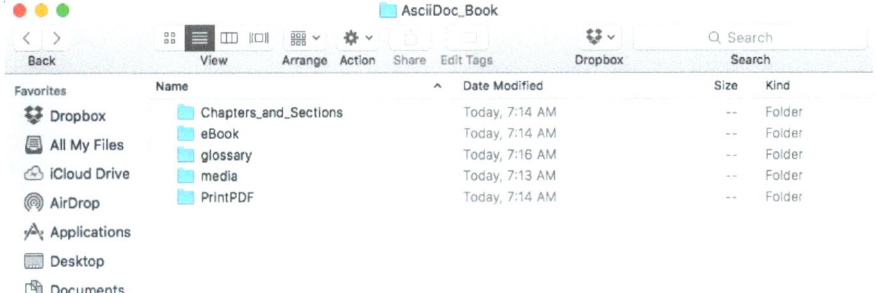

Figure 12. Initial Folder Setup

 Don't use spaces in file and folder names. It causes problems with rendering later.

Next let's make two empty plain text files. The first we'll need is the book file itself. On Windows, right click and select new, then text file, then rename it to your book's name MakeBooksFree.adoc. On a Mac, we use the command line and type touch MakeBooksFree.adoc.

No one will see this title, so make it up quickly and go. You can change your title that the public sees later.

```
touch MakeBooksFree.adoc ①
```

① The command **touch** on a Mac is how you create a new file from the terminal.

The command **touch** on a Mac is how you create a new file from the terminal.

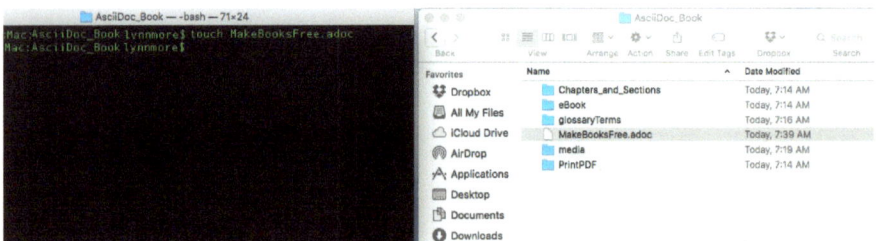

Figure 13. Add Empty Book File

 I'm using a modular approach, so the book file will not contain all your content, but is more like a map to the content files so the application knows how to render it. This associates to the lego instructions analogy I was using earlier.

Next, let's aim for a quick success by making a simple book to test that it works before we spend too much effort writing.

Let's set up a chapter with fake text, sometimes called *lorem ipsum* text just so you can see the book easily render in HTML and get a sense of how real text might be laid out. Fake text is not supposed to mean anything, but is simply intended to show where the content will be after it's written.

Open the terminal or command line and change directories to the Chapters_and_Sections folder.

```
cd Chapters_and_Sections
```

In the terminal, make a new empty file for the example content.

```
touch example1.adoc ①
```

① The command touch on a Mac is how you create a new file from the terminal.

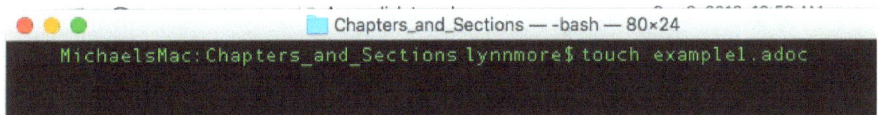

Figure 14. Creating the File for the Example Chapter With the Terminal

Write Your First Chapter

This section assumes you have already installed the Atom text editor. See Installing the Atom Text Editor.

Open this example1.adoc file using the Atom text editor, or your favorite text editor.

Add the chapter title as in the following example.

```
== Example Title for Basic Text Chapter ①
```

① The two equal signs tell the rendering app that this is a chapter title.

Now let's add some fake text. You can use blah blah blah or use lorem ipsum fake text.

 With Atom, you can wrap any text that goes off the screen using the menus **View | Toggle Soft Wrap**.

Now your file should look something like the following screenshot. I have spell check in Atom that shows the squiggly lines under all the text spelling not recognized.

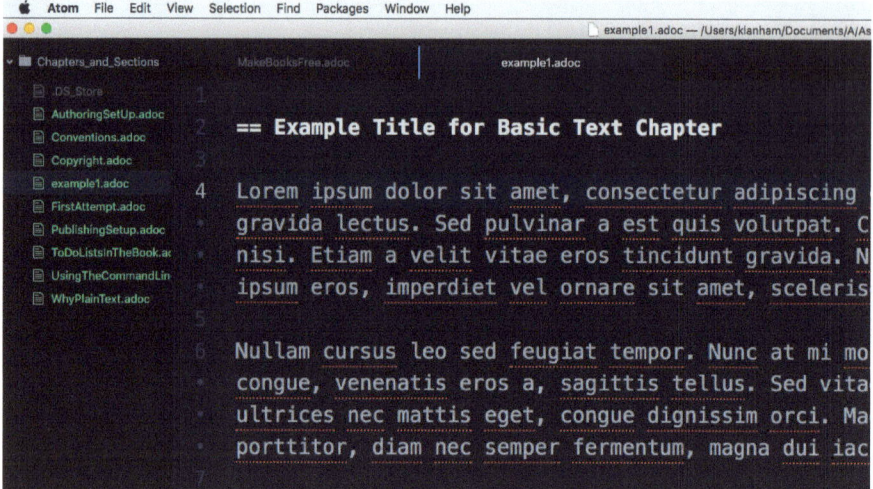

Figure 15. My Example Chapter with Lorem Ipsum Fake Text

Okay, now that we have a chapter with some content—a lego block so to speak—we need the map to tell the book to include this chapter.

Next let's edit the lego instructions, or the book map file. AsciiDoc does not really call it that, but I like the image that the term map evokes.

Change back to the main working directory.

```
cd ..
```

Open the main book file in Atom or your text editor, my book file is called MakeBooksFree.adoc. Type in a simple book.

```
                              ①
 = Make Books for Free ②
 :author: Michael Lynnmore ③

 include::Chapters_and_Sections/example1.adoc[] ④
```

① Add a blank line at the top of each *.adoc file to prevent AsciiDoctor from having errors when adding different files back together again. The blanks do not show up in the published version, but only in the source files.

② This is the book title that the readers will see. The single equal sign indicates the book title. Notice the space between the equal sign and the title.

③ The **:author:** attribute tells the rendering app that the next things are my first and last name.

④ Rather than typing all our book content into this book file directly—which you can do if you prefer that—I'm showing a modular approach where I link to the chapters. So this book file is more analogous to the lego instructions to tell the rendering app where to put all the contents for my book.

 Don't actually type the numbers (1), (2), (3), (4) at the end of each line in the preceding example. Those are for me to reference each line as I explain it to you in writting, since I'm not physically present with you to point my finger at the appropriate line.

Simple and easy. We're done "writing" a book with one chapter using AsciiDoc plain text format.

Let's now render it to HTML5 and view it in an internet browser.

 If you move the files to a different location, you have to update the **include** statements in the book file (i.e. in MakeBooksFree.adoc) to show the new path to the AsciiDoc file. Otherwise you'll break your book.

 I forgot where I read this, but add a blank line at the top of each *.adoc file before the title line so that the AsciiDoctor rendering app does not choke. I've only had a problem once in 1.5 years of using AsciiDoc. I had forgotten to add the blank line and got an error. Adding the blank line for the chapters and sections fixed the error.

Non-Recurring Setup - Rendering AsciiDoc to Other Formats

I'll start this chapter by telling you a story of a big mistake I made. I wrote an 80,000 word book. I set up my AsciiDoc authoring tools and wrote it in AsciiDoc. I figured I'd get to the publishing setup when I was done writing.

When I finished writing, and editing the book, it was time to produce it for ePub and publish on Smashwords. I had been making PDFs as I wrote, so the PDF was fine. But I needed ePub for the eBook. So I started learning how to convert the plain text into an eBook (ePub format). How hard can it be, I thought. The free app I tried was in beta and did not work for me. I got lots of errors. I had a deadline and I did not have enough time to debug such a large book to find out what I had done wrong.

This is why I now suggest iterations of writing **small batches of content** and **testing how it renders** (the production system) so that if you have a problem, you can narrow it down. You know what you just created in a period of a week or so; it is still fresh on your mind. This small batch approach avoids having months of effort that you have to dig through to find an error. I tried large batch, waiting until the end of the project and having to debug much more content to find an error I added that broke the book.

So in a hurry, I abandoned my plan to use free tools and went to Microsoft Word. I ran into issues trying to get that into an eBook. I spent days trying to figure out what was wrong before giving up on Microsoft Word. Next, I opened the Word file using Mac Pages. It turns out that Pages has a publish to ePub function. I used that, and made an ePub file. But Smashwords said there were issues so it did not go into all their network of distributors.

The lesson I learned was configure your eBook publishing at the start of the project. Use a small book, like I did for PDF, and iterate your tests until you figure out how to publish successfully to ePub. Then write the 80,000 words confident that the production process will work. I'm recommending you test all that up front so you can feel at peace it will work at the end.

Since then, I've learned how to use Sigil for creating the ePub from the HTML that AsciiDoctor renders. It is easy and reliable. My experience is what leads me to recommend that you figure out your production process at the start so you can practice it as you write.

So let's install the tools you need.

 I'll be frank. This is the point where non-technical people may lose heart and give up. Installing multiple tools can seem overwhelming to some people. I promise it is worth sticking through this part and I'll walk you through it step-by-step. You don't have to do this set up for each book project. You only have to do this set up once for each computer you buy.

Here is a list of the apps you need to set up.

- Asciidoctor
- Sigil

- PDF Tools (optional)

I will walk you through it step-by-step.

Install AsciiDoctor

WHY? You need an app to render the AsciiDoc plain text to HTML and other formats.

Asciidoctor works on Linux, OS X (Mac OS) and Windows.

1. If you did not already read Using the Command Line or Terminal, then go back and read that before continuing.

2. Open a terminal window and type in the following to check if you already have ruby installed.

```
ruby -v
```

3. If you see something like *ruby 2.2.2p95 (2015-04-13 revision 50295) [x86_64-darwin14]* then that means you already have ruby installed. Macs often already have Ruby installed.

4. If not, then you need to install ruby using the following steps.

   a. Go to the ruby installation page https://www.ruby-lang.org/en/documentation/installation/.

   b. For your operating system (Windows, MacOS, Linux), go to http://rubyinstaller.org and follow their instructions.

5. Test if your ruby installation worked by running *ruby -v* again in the terminal.

Once you have ruby installed, then we can install AsciiDoctor.

1. Ensure you have an internet connection. If you're behind a

company firewall, this is very challenging. If you're at home, it is easy.

2. Open a terminal window and type in the following.

```
gem install asciidoctor
```

3. Test if it worked by typing the following.

```
asciidoctor --version
```

4. If you see something like *Asciidoctor 1.5.4 [http://asciidoctor.org]* then it was successful.

 On Windows, you have to be in the directory folder where you installed the asciidoctor app for it to run.

Install Sigil

WHY? You need an app to correctly save your book content into the picky format of eBooks. This app makes it easy.

I have found Sigil to be the easiest eBook tool to use with a bit of initial guidance. It is not obvious what to do with it the first time however, so I'll tell you how.

1. Go to https://sigil-ebook.com to read about the app.

2. To download, go to https://github.com/Sigil-Ebook/Sigil/releases and scroll down to the downloads section.

3. You should see a list of options (the version number 0.9.6 may change):

- Sigil-0.9.6-Mac-Package.dmg

- Sigil-0.9.6-Windows-Setup.exe

- Sigil-0.9.6-Windows-x64-Setup.exe

4. Determine if your machine is 32-bit or 64-bit. Most new machines are 64-bit processors in 2017.

   a. For Windows OS, View the System window in Control Panel.

   b. Click Start, and then click Run.

   c. Type sysdm.cpl, and then click OK.

   d. Click the General tab. The operating system is displayed as follows: For a 64-bit version operating system, Windows XP Professional x64 Edition Version < Year> appears under System.

   e. If MacOS, click on the Apple menu and then choose About This Mac.

   f. Locate the Processor Name.

   g. Ask Google if the processor name is 64 bit.

5. Select the Sigil download package that works for your platform. If Mac, use the .dmg. If windows 64 bit machine, select the Windows-x64-Setup.exe version.

6. Follow normal methods for installing a dmg on Mac or an exe file on Windows.

7. Look up on Google if you're not sure.

Install PDF Tools

WHY? You need these tools if you want to create PDF files to go to print for your book.

Installing PDF tools is entirely **optional**. If you only plan to produce eBooks using ePub or Amazon's format, you don't need the ability to render to PDF. I'm using PDF is just to go to print using print on demand providers like https://www.createspace.com.

 If you get stuck trying to install Java on your computer, go to Youtube and look for videos of people doing it. You may have an easier time of it following someone's video instructions.

1. Download the Java Development Kit (JDK), which includes the Java runtime (and, naturally, an internet connection). You can use any recent JDK.

   a. Go to Java SE download site @ http://www.oracle.com/technetwork/java/javase/downloads/index.html.

   b. Under "Java Platform, Standard Edition" find "Java SE 8" or 9, and click the "JDK Download" button.

   c. Check "Accept License Agreement".

   d. Choose your operating platform, e.g., "Windows x64" (for 64-bit Windows OS) or "Windows x86" (for 32-bit Windows OS).

2. Install the JDK.

   a. Run the downloaded installer, the *.dmg (Mac) or *.exe (Windows) that you just downloaded (e.g., "jdk-8u{xx}-windows-x64.exe")

   b. Accept the defaults.

   c. Follow the screen instructions to install JDK and JRE.

   d. Check the JDK installed directory by inspecting these folders using File Explorer.

e. Take note of your JDK installed directory, which you will need in the next step.

3. Verify the JDK Installation

   a. Launch a terminal or command line window.

   b. Type the following.

```
java -version
```

   c. If you see something like java version "1.8.0_xx", Java™ SE Runtime Environment, then you succeeded.

4. Install the asciidoctor-fopub app.

   a. Create a folder called asciidoctor-fopub. I put mine here, Users/lynnmore/Documents/A/asciidoctor-fopub.

   b. Go to https://github.com/asciidoctor/asciidoctor-fopub.

   c. Look for the download button on the right-hand side of the repository page on GitHub.

   d. Select the download button and then select **Download ZIP**.

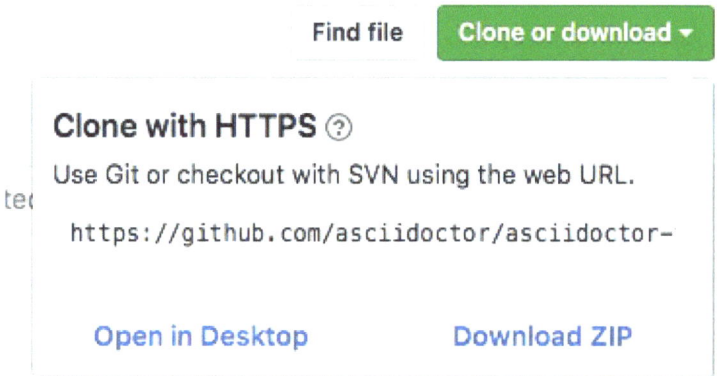

Figure 16. Asciidoctor-fopub App Download Button

e. Once the download finishes, move the zip file to the asciidoctor-fopub folder you made.

f. Extract the archive in the asciidoctor-fopub folder.

g. Open a terminal or command line window and change to the book working folder directory using cd command followed by the file path.

5. Test that the asciidoctor-fopub app works.

Your First Attempt Rendering to HTML5

Okay, now that you have a written draft of your book (using fake text to test rendering), let's render it to HTML5 because that is the easiest output.

This portion assumes you have already have installed AsciiDoctor as shown in Install AsciiDoctor.

Open the terminal and enter the command below to render to HTML5.

```
asciidoctor -b html5 MakeBooksFree.adoc
```

Go to your work folder and look for MakeBooksFree.html, my file's name. Open that file in an internet browser by dragging the file into the browser or using the browser's **File | Open** menus.

Your newly rendered fake chapter should appear as follows.

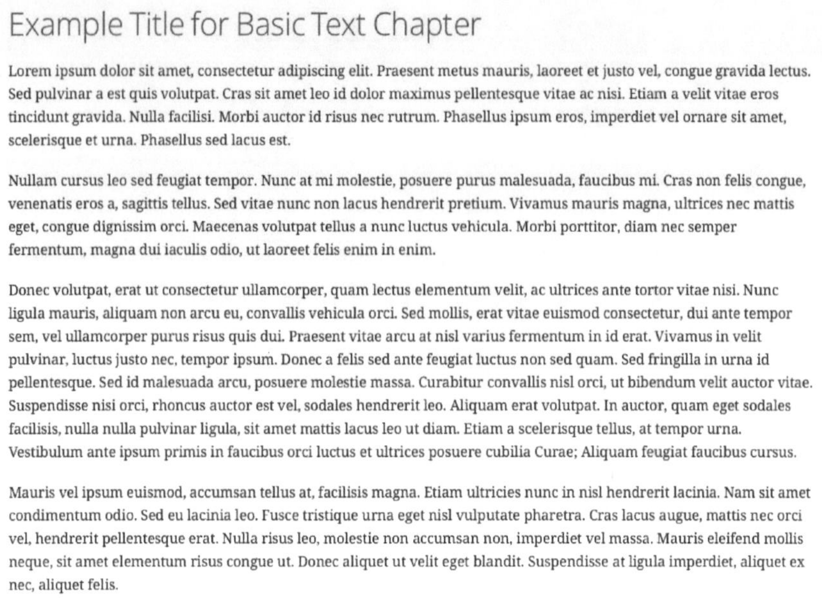

Example Title for Basic Text Chapter

Lorem ipsum dolor sit amet, consectetur adipiscing elit. Praesent metus mauris, laoreet et justo vel, congue gravida lectus. Sed pulvinar a est quis volutpat. Cras sit amet leo id dolor maximus pellentesque vitae ac nisi. Etiam a velit vitae eros tincidunt gravida. Nulla facilisi. Morbi auctor id risus nec rutrum. Phasellus ipsum eros, imperdiet vel ornare sit amet, scelerisque et urna. Phasellus sed lacus est.

Nullam cursus leo sed feugiat tempor. Nunc at mi molestie, posuere purus malesuada, faucibus mi. Cras non felis congue, venenatis eros a, sagittis tellus. Sed vitae nunc non lacus hendrerit pretium. Vivamus mauris magna, ultrices nec mattis eget, congue dignissim orci. Maecenas volutpat tellus a nunc luctus vehicula. Morbi porttitor, diam nec semper fermentum, magna dui iaculis odio, ut laoreet felis enim in enim.

Donec volutpat, erat ut consectetur ullamcorper, quam lectus elementum velit, ac ultrices ante tortor vitae nisi. Nunc ligula mauris, aliquam non arcu eu, convallis vehicula orci. Sed mollis, erat vitae euismod consectetur, dui ante tempor sem, vel ullamcorper purus risus quis dui. Praesent vitae arcu at nisl varius fermentum in id erat. Vivamus in velit pulvinar, luctus justo nec, tempor ipsum. Donec a felis sed ante feugiat luctus non sed quam. Sed fringilla in urna id pellentesque. Sed id malesuada arcu, posuere molestie massa. Curabitur convallis nisl orci, ut bibendum velit auctor vitae. Suspendisse nisi orci, rhoncus auctor est vel, sodales hendrerit leo. Aliquam erat volutpat. In auctor, quam eget sodales facilisis, nulla nulla pulvinar ligula, sit amet mattis lacus leo ut diam. Etiam a scelerisque tellus, at tempor urna. Vestibulum ante ipsum primis in faucibus orci luctus et ultrices posuere cubilia Curae; Aliquam feugiat faucibus cursus.

Mauris vel ipsum euismod, accumsan tellus at, facilisis magna. Etiam ultricies nunc in nisl hendrerit lacinia. Nam sit amet condimentum odio. Sed eu lacinia leo. Fusce tristique urna eget nisl vulputate pharetra. Cras lacus augue, mattis nec orci vel, hendrerit pellentesque erat. Nulla risus leo, molestie non accumsan non, imperdiet vel massa. Mauris eleifend mollis neque, sit amet elementum risus congue ut. Donec aliquet ut velit eget blandit. Suspendisse at ligula imperdiet, aliquet ex nec, aliquet felis.

Figure 17. Rendered to HTML

Congratulations!

If you had perhaps been one of those people who thought this method was too hard to use, then now consider that typing **one command** in the terminal to make HTML **is easy** not hard. You also had to learn how to use Microsoft Word at one time.

Let's Add Images to Your Book

Your first iteration was successful. Now let's do another iteration and add on some more capability.

As easy as the first iteration was, a text-only book might not be enough for your needs. You might like to add images. So let's see how to do that.

Adding using AsciiDoc is easy. So let's walk through it step-by-step.

If I asked you where your car keys are now, could you tell me their location without actually giving the keys to me? Yes.

Well, that is the approach we'll use for adding images. Instead of dragging and dropping like you do in word processing applications, we'll just tell the AsciiDoc file where the image is located. That's it. When it renders, the rendering app goes and gets the image and adds it right where you told it to add the image.

Let's use an example. Let's go back to the example chapter you just finished and add an image after the first paragraph. The following is the AsciiDoc source I'm adding to get the image.

```
Here is a new paragraph, below which I'm adding my image.
①
②
.My Silly "Fake Text" Image ③
image::media\FakeTextImage.png[] ④
⑤
Here is the next new paragraph. Blah blah blah blah blah.
Blah blah blah blah blah blah blah blah. Blah blah blah
blah.
```

① A new paragraph added to discuss the image

② A line break between the preceding paragraph and the image block

③ The figure caption goes after the period with no spaces.

④ The **image::** identifier tells the render app to find the image file at the path that follows. In this case the file path is media\FakeTextImage.png. The square brackets at the end tell the rendering app that the image path is done.

⑤ A line break between the image block and the following paragraph

 Please notice that I have not allocated any time to improving my graphic artist skills. This poor graphic is my attempt to show an example image, and I did it with a picture of text.

That's it. You did it. The render app goes and gets the image where you told it and puts it right here. The following is this new content rendered so you can see how it comes out.

Example Title for Basic Text Chapter

Lorem ipsum dolor sit amet, consectetur adipiscing elit. Praesent metus mauris, laoreet et justo vel, congue gravida lectus. Sed pulvinar a est quis volutpat. Cras sit amet leo id dolor maximus pellentesque vitae ac nisi. Etiam a velit vitae eros tincidunt gravida. Nulla facilisi. Morbi auctor id risus nec rutrum. Phasellus ipsum eros, imperdiet vel ornare sit amet, scelerisque et urna. Phasellus sed lacus est.

Here is a new paragraph, below which I'm adding my image.

Figure 1. My Silly "Fake Text" Image

Here is the next new paragraph. Blah blah blah blah blah. Blah blah blah blah blah blah blah blah. Blah blah blah blah.

Nullam cursus leo sed feugiat tempor. Nunc at mi molestie, posuere purus malesuada, faucibus mi. Cras non felis congue, venenatis eros a, sagittis tellus. Sed vitae nunc non lacus hendrerit pretium. Vivamus mauris magna, ultrices nec mattis

Figure 18. Example File With an Image

Making Screen Capture Images

To capture images from your screen for your book, there are two free tools I recommend depending on your system.

- Greenshot app for Windows (http://getgreenshot.org/) is my favorite on Windows OS

- Command + Shift + 4 for Mac (it is a built in screen capture utility for MacOS)

Editing Images

There are two great free tools for editing images. For raster graphics, the app called Gimp is terrific. It is a free replacement of Photoshop.

For vector graphics, a good tool is Inkscape.

These both work for all platforms.

Image Resolution

Images designed for use on a web page or eBook can be 72 dpi resolution, but images intended for printing with a PDF file need to be 300-600 dpi resolution.

Use an image editing app, such as GIMP, to edit the resolution of images. The publishing app will take exactly what you give it.

So check your PDF and HTML versions carefully. If your PDF images are going off the page, you will need to change their size to fit within your paper margins at the desired resolution.

If your images seem blocky you might have tried to increase a 72 dpi image to 300 dpi or more for print. A good rule of thumb is that you can start with high resolution images and edit easily to lower resolution, but you cannot go from low resolution images to high resolution images without losing image clarity.

Let's Add a Cross Reference

Sometimes in nonfiction writing we need a cross reference between one part of the book to another part of the book. We can easily add cross references using AsciiDoc plain text.

First, I'll show you an example of the cross reference start point. In this book, in the "Gotchas" chapter, I have cross referenced to the audio review chapter. Here is the cross reference **start point** in this book's AsciiDoc source text.

```
When using audio review (see <<audioReview>>), if you
hear ①
```

① The cross reference start point is a code of your choosing surrounded by double angle brackets.

Next, I'll show you how to add the cross reference **target**.

```
[[audioReview]] ①
== The Secret to Nearly Free Reviews ②
```

① The cross reference target is a code of your choosing surrounded by **double** square brackets.

② The location of the cross reference target should be near where you want the reader to link. Here I added it immediately before the chapter title.

If the code you type for the cross reference start point doesn't **exactly match** the cross reference target, the cross reference link will be broken because the rendering app won't know where to make the link. This link code must also be the **exact same case** (UPPER case or lower case letters).

Rather than complicated codes, I just use a phrase for the target and jam the words all together and use what's called *camel case*. This means the first word is lowercase and each additional word is initial cap.

In many apps programming rules apply, meaning that adding spaces in codes or link identifiers causes problems. To avoid this group of problems I avoid spaces in identifiers for cross references. Camel case removes the spaces.

So, for example if my target is about dogs being cute, then I might want to use the phrase "Dogs are cute" and I'd translate it to "dogAreCute" as my cross reference code.

You can use whatever you'd like to use as long as the two codes match so the rendering app can link between the start point and the target or end point.

The preceding example renders as follows.

When using audio review (see The Secret to Nearly Free Reviews), if you hear

Figure 19. Cross Reference Example

Let's Add Footnotes

Sometimes in nonfiction writing, we need to add footnotes. We can easily add footnotes using AsciiDoc plain text.

AsciiDoc is nice because it frees the author from having to worry about a numbering scheme for footnotes. AsciiDoctor renders the footnote number references automatically.

Footnotes Used Only One Time

Let's look at a footnote example in AsciiDoc.

```
footnote:[Your footnote text goes here.]
```

It is okay if your footnote text spans multiple lines.

How to Add Footnotes

1. Add the key word "footnote".

2. Add a colon ":".

3. Add square brackets.

4. Type your footnote text into the square brackets.

5. Render your AsciiDoc to HTML if you'd like to see that the footnote rendered as you expected.

6. Look at the bottom of the page on PDFs or at the end of the book in HTML to find your footnote text.

Here is a **correct** footnote example. [15: An example footnote only] Follow the footnote reference to confirm it works.

Here is an incorrect footnote example.footnote[An example footnote only] where I forgot to use the colon after the footnote keyword.

If you combine the key word, the colon, and the square brackets, it works every time.

See Footnote Problems for an example of how to recover from a typical mistake.

Footnotes Used Multiple Times

Sometimes you need to use a footnote that may be referenced multiple times. To avoid the rendering app from adding the same note over and over in the footnotes section, AsciiDoc provides a way that when a reference must be repeated the footnote indicator can be repeated in the text without repeating the footnote itself.

 Consult your style guide to determine how many pages of content can go by before the first reference is too far away and a new footnote better serves the reader.

Let's say I'm using a bullet list where I need to provide attribution to two different list items. Here is how I could do that in AsciiDoc.

```
* list item so and so footnoteref:[Washington, Used by
permission from John T. Washington.] ①
* list item thus and thus
* list item next
* list item next after that footnoteref:[Washington] ②
```

① The first time uses the footnoteref key word, and it uses a code you make up and a comma separator before your footnote content.

② The second or more times also uses the footnoteref key word, but it only shows the code you made up in the first instance.

 The code you make up for multiple footnotes must match each time you reference the initial footnote.

 When using multiple footnotes, the first instance must include the footnote content. If later you add another instance above the one with the content (see callout 1 in the preceding example), then you have to move the full multiple footnote to a location before the other multiple references.

For example, the wrong way is shown in the following example.

```
* My new list item added after the other footnotes
footnoteref:[Washington] ①
* list item so and so footnoteref:[Washington, Used by
permission from John T. Washington.] ②
* list item thus and thus
* list item next
* list item next after that footnoteref:[Washington] ③
```

① The multiple footnote reference I added later is now broken because it is before the first use with the footnote content in line 2.

② This full multiple footnote instance has to come before all the other references.

③ This instance will still work because it is below the full version in line 2.

Let's Add Index Entries for Print

There are debates over whether indexing is still needed. Print books still need them to find contents. However, many digital books include full text search and this caused some to argue that indexes are no longer needed. I think they help readers.

With the free tools I'm recommending you'll only get a back-of-the-book index for PDF because its intended for printing to paper books. There are other free tools like the DocBook chain of XML tools, but that requires a skill level you may not want to work to achieve, so I'll leave that out. Just know that if you must include an index for eBooks you'll need to use DocBook's approach.

There are two ways of adding index entries.

```
1. indexterm:[primary, secondary, tertiary] ①

2. (((primary, secondary, tertiary))) ②
```

① This type of index entry only shows up in the index, not in the book content.

② This type of index entry shows the text inside to the reader in the content and in the index.

Here is an index entry example from this book.

```
Often nonfiction books need a glossary.
AsciiDoc makes it easy to ((add a glossary)). ①
```

① This primary index entry is inline and the text inside is both rendered for the reader and added to the index for PDF. You know its a primary entry because there are no other index entries inside the double parentheses separated by commas.

For people not familiar with indexing conventions, sometimes one index entry has several subentries.

```
table
    adding rows
    adding columns
    spanning cells
```

To accomplish this in AsciiDoc, you would need to use primary and secondary entries. See the following example.

```
Let's talk about how to make table rows.
indexterm:[table, adding rows]
```

The rendering app, AsciiDoctor, takes these inline index entries and adds a page number in the index for wherever the page this content shows up. Having the tool automatically generate an index entry frees the author to not worry about such things as long as the index entries are formatted correctly.

The primary index entry is table in the preceding example. One of the secondary index entry is "adding rows", which typically is indented under the primary entry.

It is important to get all the primary entries correct or you'll have a messy index. For this reason, many indexes include mostly primary index entries only. That is the case with this book.

Let's Add Glossary Terms

Often nonfiction books need a glossary. AsciiDoc makes it easy to add a glossary. By way of example, let's define glossary and term so you can see how asciidoctor renders a glossary term.

glossary

> An alphabetical list of terms or words found in or relating to a specific subject, text, or dialect, with explanations; a brief dictionary.

term

> A word or phrase used to describe a thing or to express a concept, especially in a particular kind of language or branch of study.

The Easy Way—Inline

You can include a glossary of terms and definitions by including the [glossary] marker before the section header.

```
[glossary] ①
== Glossary ②

draft:: ③
    The book's content at a particular point in time.
Typically a first draft is followed by later drafts. The
final draft is self-published. ④

draft:: The book's content at a particular point in time.
Typically a first draft is followed by later drafts. The
final draft is self-published. ⑤
```

① The glossary marker for asciidoctor to identify this section as the glossary.

② The chapter or section title (depends on the number of equal signs you use).

③ The term, separated by double colons "::"

④ The definition.

⑤ Although you can stuff both the term and the definition all on the same line, it makes the AsciiDoc plain text file harder for humans to read.

A Harder Way to Organize Glossary Terms for Reuse

AsciiDoc also makes it easy to reuse a glossary entry (a term + its definition) from a small text file. This is how I use glossary terms.

If you're just writing one book, there is no need for this.

```
=== E ①

include::ebook.adoc[] ②
```

① My book's glossary is separated by letter headings.

② I use the asciidoctor "include::" command to tell the rendering app to include everthing in that text file called draft.adoc.

Inside that separate file, I have only my term and its definition.

```
eBook::
   An electronic version of a book that is read using
mobile devices with reader apps or on a laptop or desktop
if a reader app is installed. It is essentially a self-
contained website in a zip file.
```

I include a blank line before each glossary entry (term +
definition) so they don't run together when rendered all in the
same location.

This allows me to organize all my glossary entries in a single
folder.

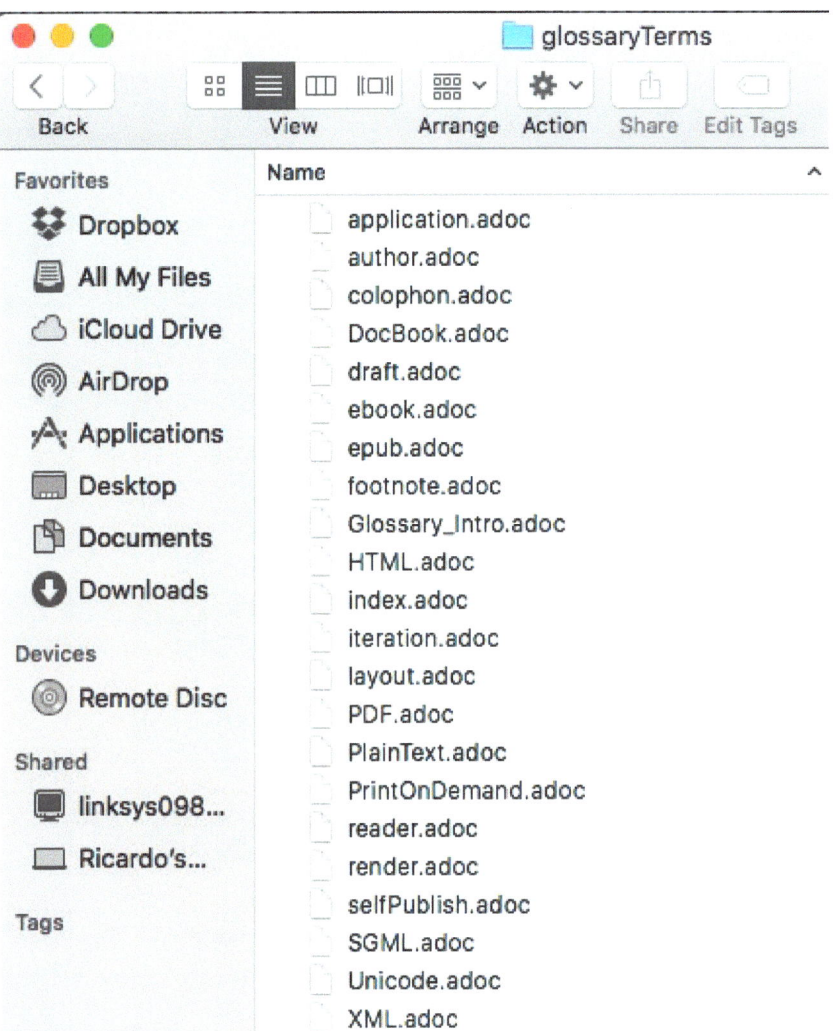

Figure 20. Glossary Files

And it still renders all together.

draft

The book's content at a particular point in time. Typically a first draft is followed by later drafts. The final draft is self-published.

E

ebook

An electronic version of a book that is read using mobile devices with reader apps or on a laptop or desktop if a reader app is installed. It is essentially a self-contained website in a zip file.

Figure 21. HTML Version of Glossary Entry

And finally, this method of glossary chunking allows me to have a single source for definitions that can be referenced in the book in multiple places if necessary.

A Book Skeleton

So let's look at how the whole book structure might look if you're doing it all in one monolithic document file. It took me a while to figure this out, so I'll show you by example.

```
= Book Title Here
:author: Your Name
:email: myemail.address@mydomain.com
:authorinitials: XX
:revnumber: 1.0
:revremark: Incorporated reviewer comments
:revdate: 2016-09-24
:sectnums:
:icons: font
:toc: left
:toclevels: 2
// This is the end of the attributes section.
// Leave no line breaks between attributes.

[dedication]
== Dedication
For so and so, blah blah blah.

[preface]
== Preface
Blah blah blah.

== Chapter 1 Title Goes Here
Blah blah blah.

== Chapter 2 Title Goes Here
Blah blah blah.

[colophon]
== Colophon
```

```
Blah blah blah.

[glossary]
== Glossary

[appendix]
== Extra Stuff Not in the Main Book
Blah blah blah.

[index]
== Index Terms
// The index contents are generated automatically
```

If you decide on a modular approach, then the book skeleton is less and the details are in the files of each chunk being added by the "include::" command.

```
= Book Title Here
:author: Your Name
:email: myemail.address@mydomain.com
:authorinitials: KL
:revnumber: 1.0
:revremark: Incorporated reviewer comments
:revdate: 2016-09-24
:sectnums:
:icons: font
:toc: left
:toclevels: 2
// This is the end of the attributes section.
// Leave no line breaks between attributes.

// Here begins the references to the content files.
// Include a blank line between each to help the
rendering app, AsciiDoctor.

include::Chapters_and_Sections\Dedication.adoc[]
```

```
include::Chapters_and_Sections\Preface.adoc[]

include::Chapters_and_Sections\YourFileNameForChapter1.ad
oc[]

include::Chapters_and_Sections\YourFileNameForChapter2.ad
oc[]

include::Chapters_and_Sections\Colophon.adoc[]

include::glossaryTerms\Glossary.adoc[]

include::Chapters_and_Sections\AppendixA.adoc[]

[index]
== Index Terms
// The index contents are generated automatically
```

By comparing and contrasting these two approaches you can see which better meets your needs.

Make a PDF for Print

Sometimes you need a PDF file to sent a fixed format document to a printer. This section shows you how.

1. Open a terminal window.

2. Type the following command.

   ```
   asciidoctor -b docbook -d book -a data-uri!
   MakeBooksFree.adoc
   ```

3. Check your working directory and see if a file called MakeBooksFree.xml now exists.

4. Change to the directory that the fopub app is located in.

   ```
   cd /Users/lynnmore/Documents/A/asciidoctor-fopub
   ```

5. Type the fopub app name and the book path and filename.

   ```
   ./fopub
   /Users/lynnmore/Documents/A/AsciiDoc_Book/MakeBooksFr
   ee.xml
   ```

6. Check that MakeBooksFree.pdf now exists.

7. Review the MakeBooksFree.pdf file for correctness.

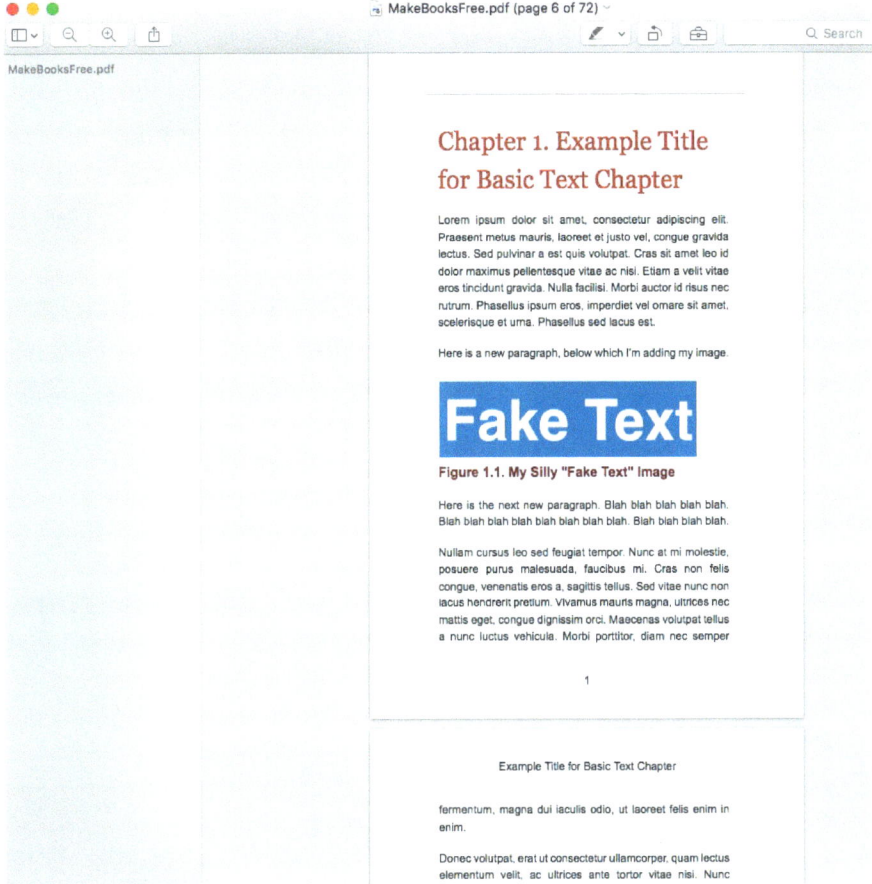

Figure 22. The PDF Worked

The folder location makes all the difference for the admonishment graphics to show up.

If you're using conditional publishing, then in the book file flip the attribute switch to either :printedVersion: and //:epubHTML: or the reverse //:printedVersion: and :epubHTML: or some other code you invent for rendering your content conditionally. You can make up whatever code you like as long as they are different from each other.

Make an eBook

To make and eBook, we'll first make an HTML version of the AsciiDoc plain text files using the AsciiDoctor app. Then we'll add that HTML file into an eBook making app, called Sigil. We'll make an eBook cover, or check the dimensions of a cover someone else makes for you. The following instructions walk you through how to make an eBook step-by-step.

Convert the AsciiDoc Content into HTML

1. Open a terminal window (Mac) or Command Prompt (Windows).

2. Type the following command to render the AsciiDoc plain text source to HTML.

```
asciidoctor -b html5 MakeBooksFree.adoc
```

3. Open the book file, for me is MakeBooksFree.html, that AsciiDoctor made automatically and check it is as expected.

Make an eBook Cover

We need an eBook cover. You can pay someone to make one for you or you can make your own.

Your eBook cover should be a graphic image sized approximately 1,600 pixels wide by 2,400 pixels tall.

Free tools include:

Gimp (for raster images)

- Inkscape (for vector images)

I prefer Gimp.

1. Follow installation instructions for your computer from https://www.gimp.org.

2. Open Gimp.

3. Open your cover file.

4. Go to **Image** | **Scale Image**.

5. Modify the scale in pixels to near the ideal eBook cover size of 1600 px X 2400 px high.

6. When done, use **File** | **Export** to save the cover to a PNG or JPG file.

Make EPUB Format eBook for all Readers Except Kindle

1. Open the Sigil app on your computer.

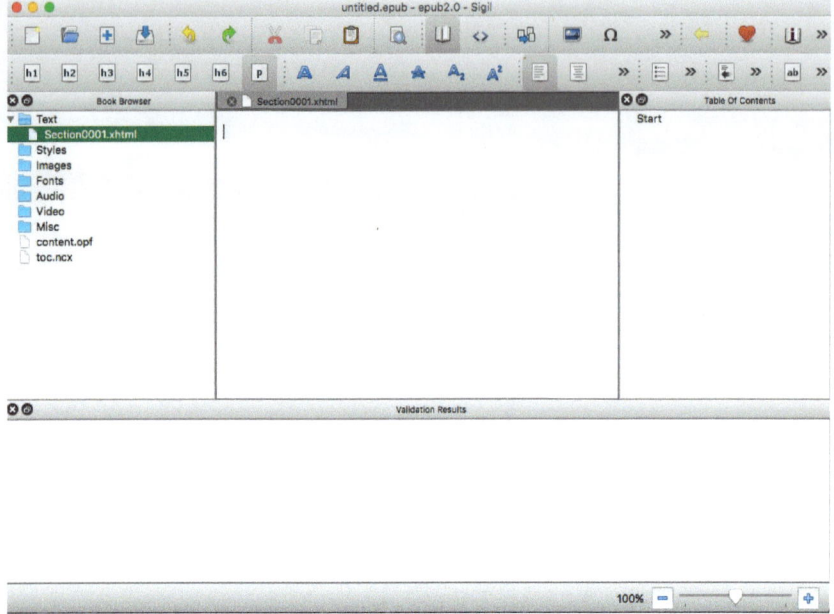

Figure 23. Opening Screen for Sigil

2. Ignore most of what you see.

3. Select the Text folder as shown.

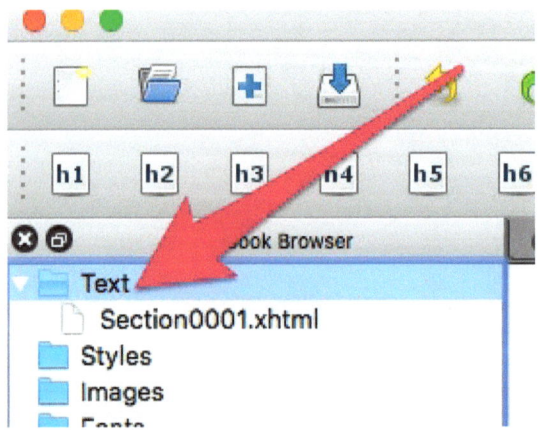

4. Select **File | Add | Existing Files** as shown.

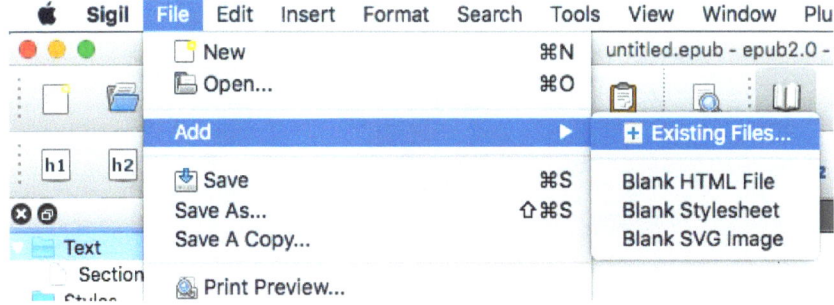

5. Navigate to your working folder where you have the book files and select the book file HTML version, for my book is MakeBooksFree.html. This screenshot shows using the add existing file icon rather than the file menus.

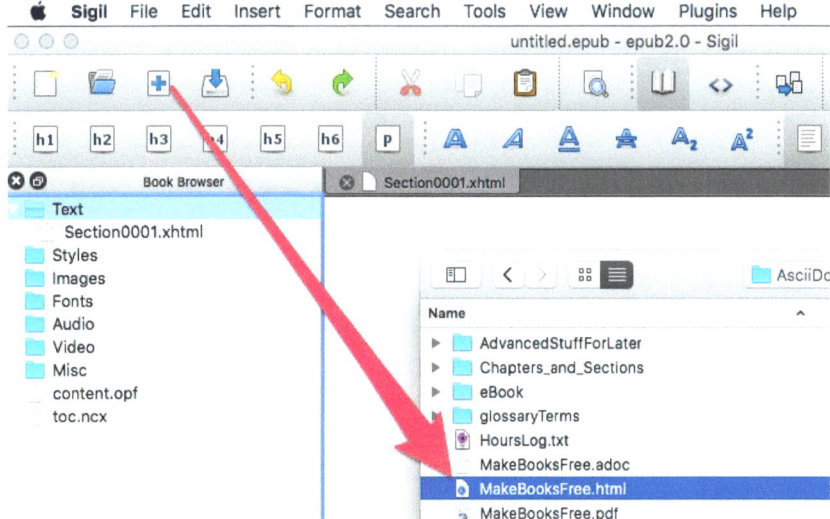

6. Check that your book file was added. See in the example how MakeBooksFree.html now shows up.

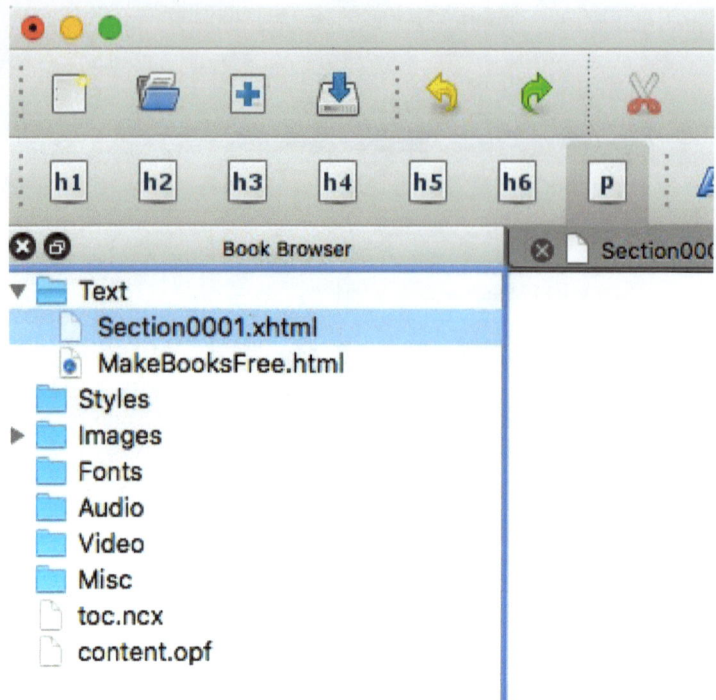

7. Select the default file that was included in Sigil, called Section0001.xhtml, and press your delete key. The *Delete Files* window pops up with the Section0001.xhtml file checked.

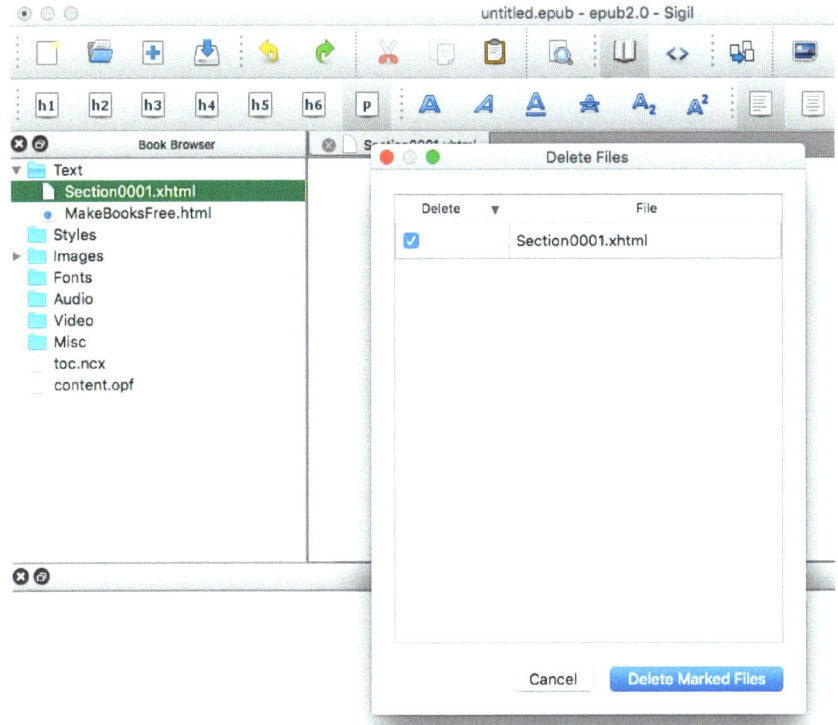

8. Confirm Section0001.xhtml shows in the delete window and select **Delete Marked Files** button at the bottom of the *Delete Files* window.

9. The default file should disappear, leaving only your book file.

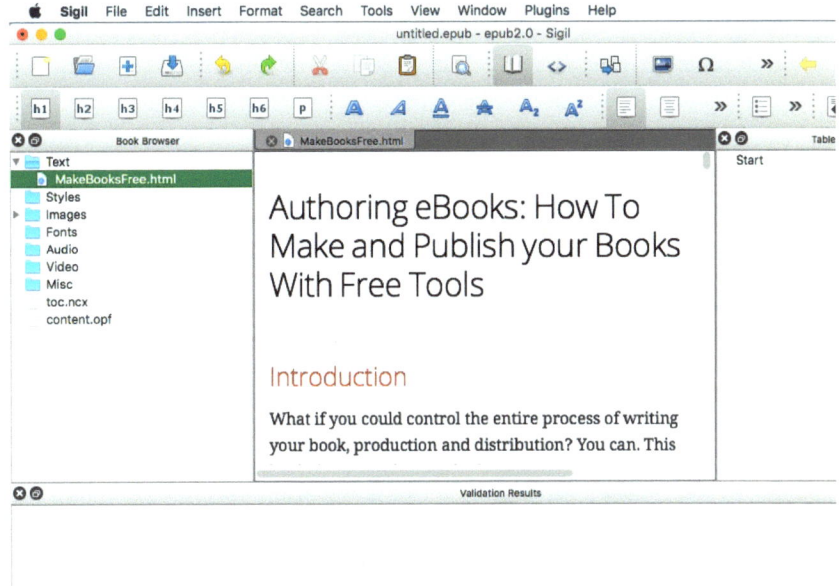

10. Select **Tools** | **Table of Contents** | **Generate Table of Contents**

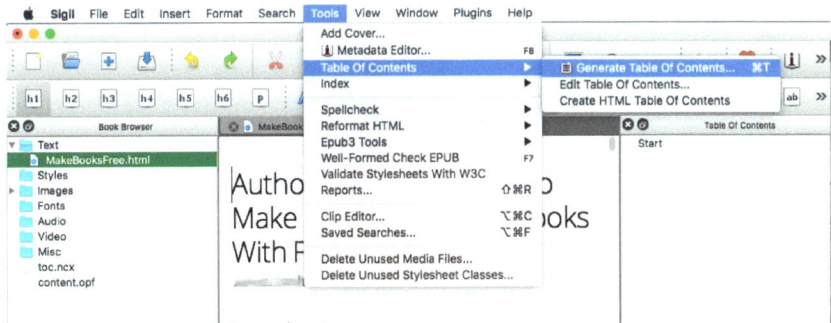

11. Select the titles you don't want in the Table of Contents and they disappear. In my screenshot example, I'm removing all the h3 titles so my TOC is not too cluttered.

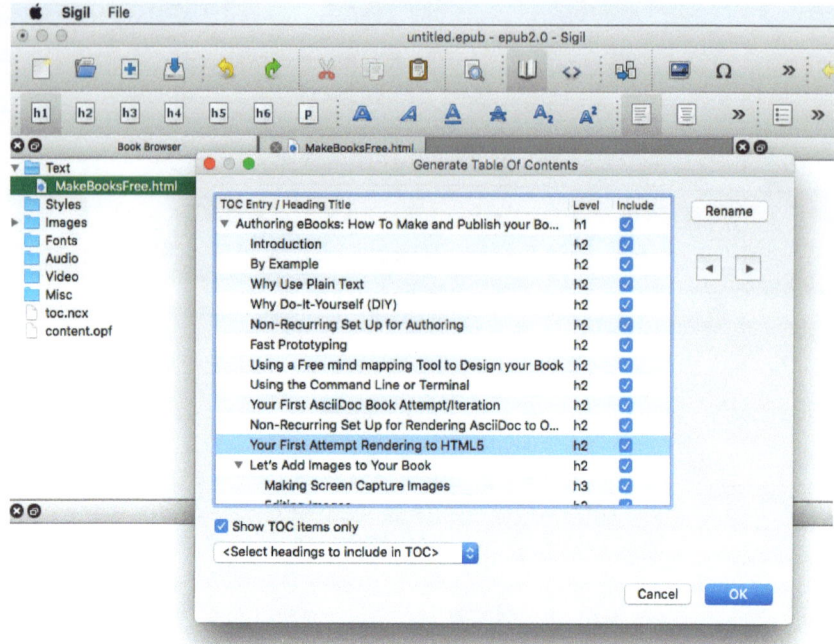

12. Select the **OK** button and the eBook table of contents is automatically generated.

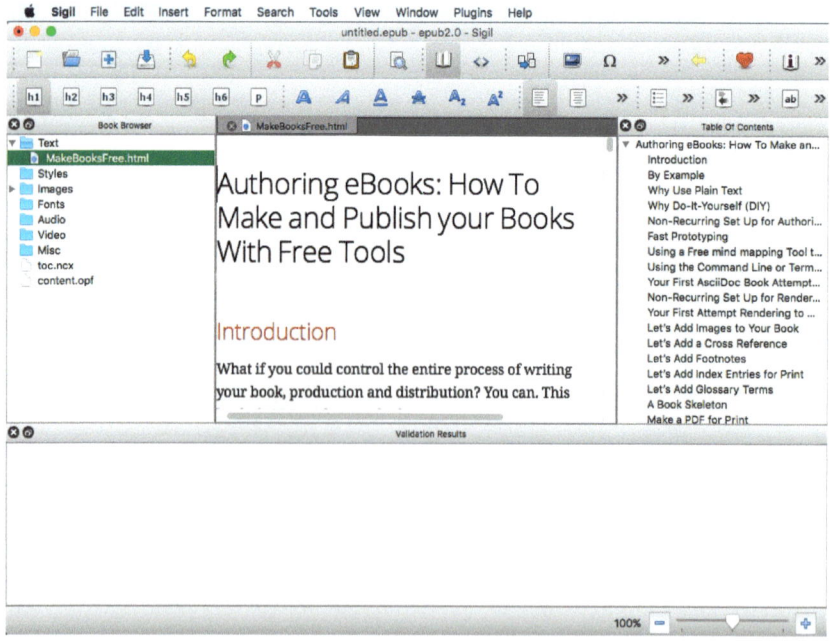

Select **Tools | Add Cover**.

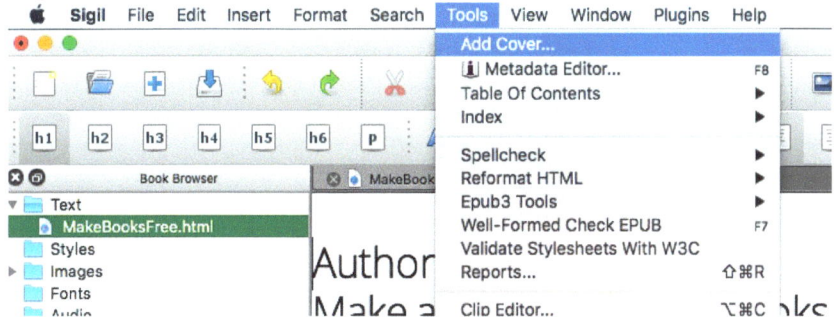

14. The cover image selector window opens. Select your cover graphic file and select **OK**.

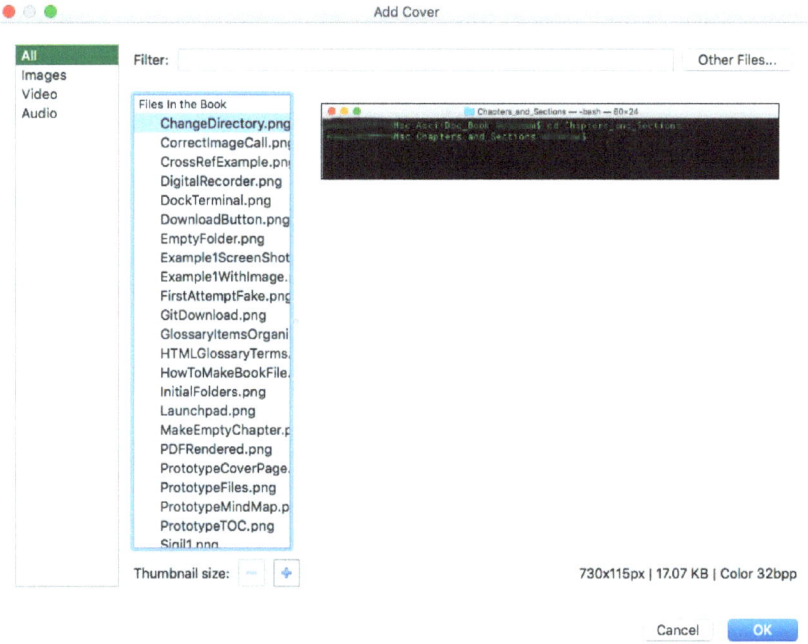

15. Your cover should show up as a new tab in the middle pane of Sigil as shown.

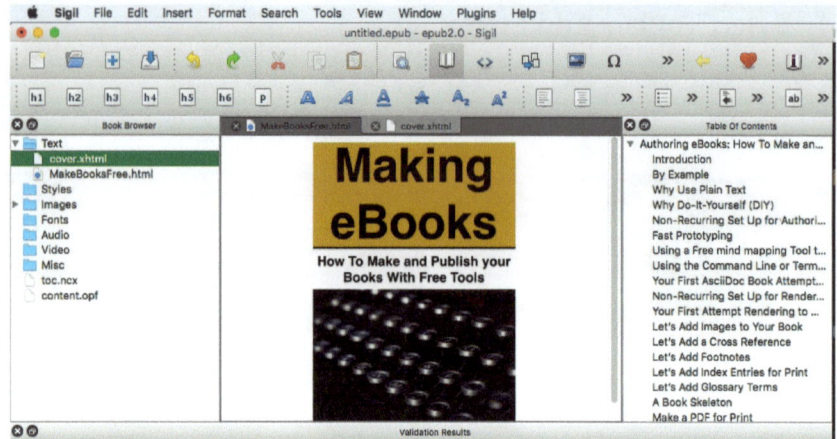

16. Select **Tools | Well Formed Check EPUB** to validate your eBook.

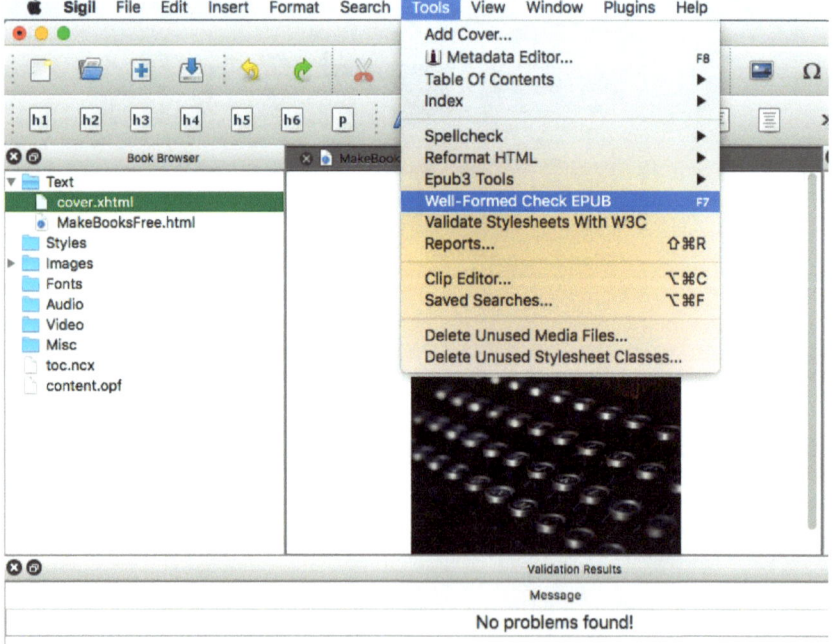

17. Check that the validation results pane message shows "No problems found."

18. Select **Tools | Metadata Editor** to add metadata to your eBook.

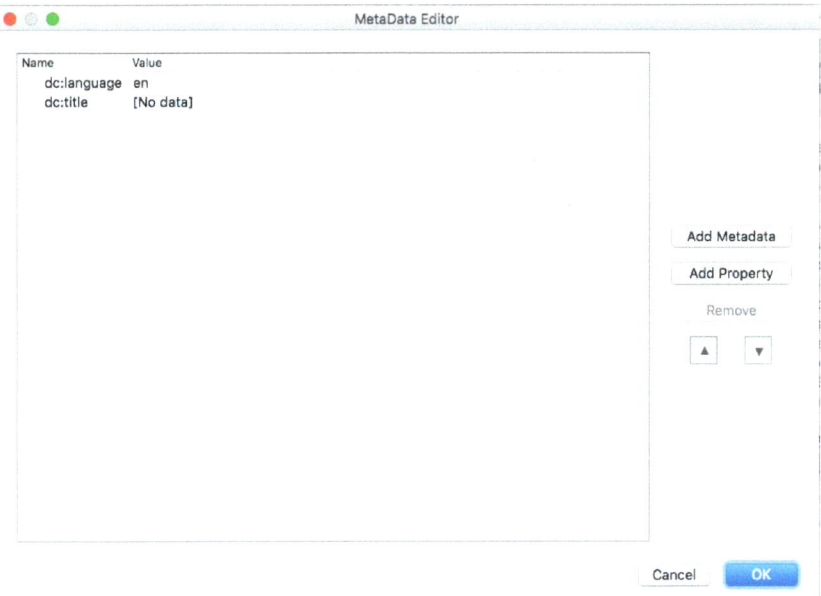

19. Select **Add Metadata** and select the metadata type you want to add. For example, Author.

20. Click on the field that shows **[No Data]**, and type in what you want instead.

21. When done adding metadata select the **OK** button.

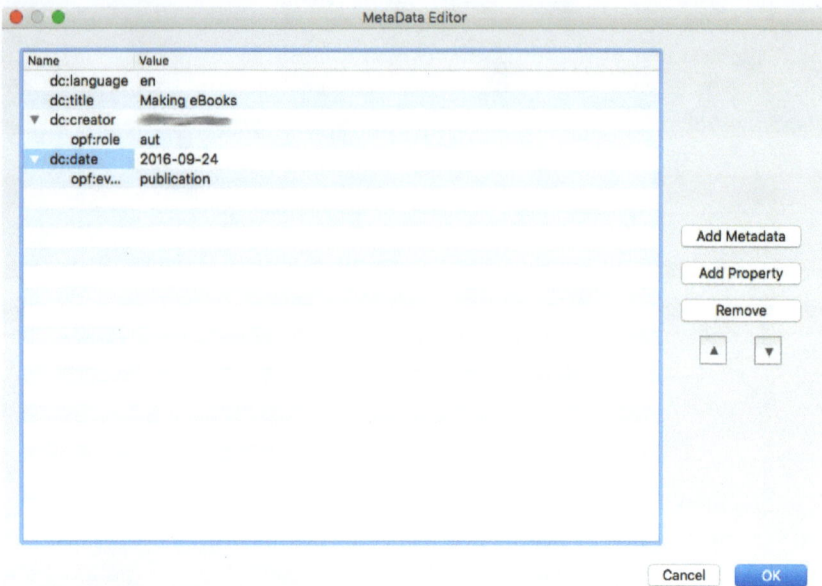

22. Select **File | Save As**.

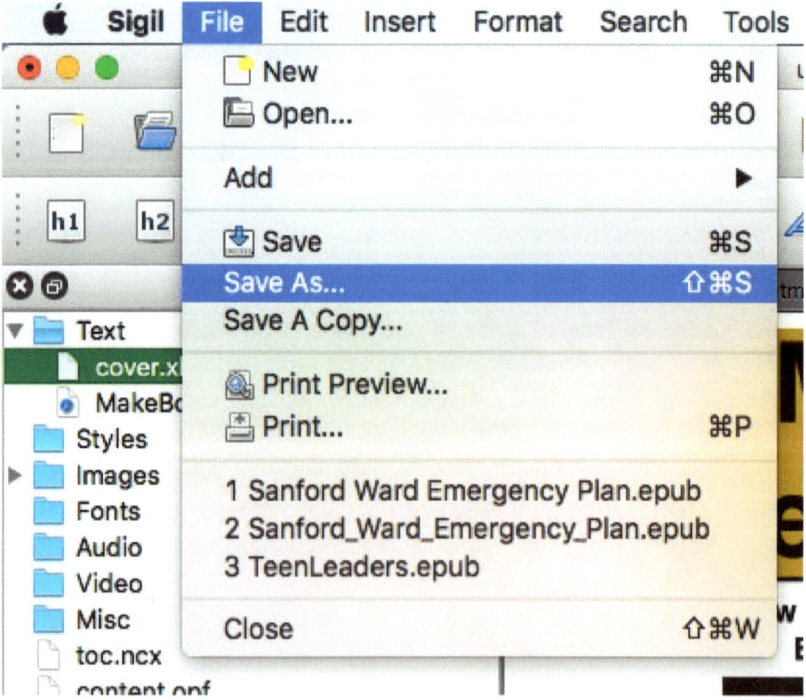

23. Add the filename for your eBook then select **Save**.

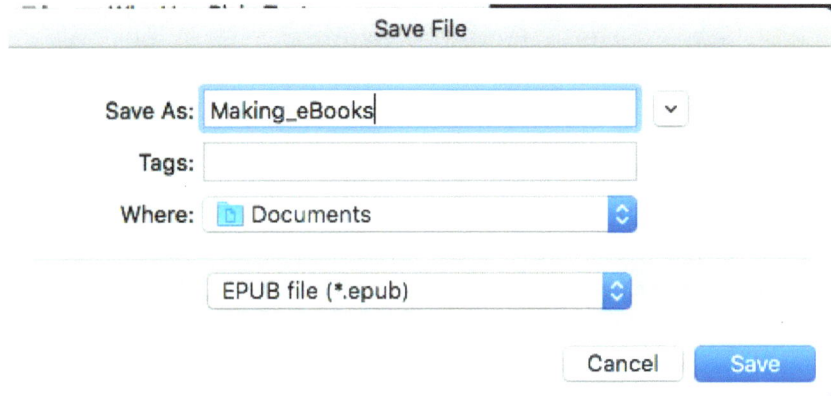

24. Close the Sigil app.

Congratulations, you made an ePub eBook.

Make Amazon Format eBook for Kindle

Although ePub is the most common ebook format, Amazon decided to make their own format. This means that Kindle readers can't read ePub without an easy conversion to Mobi or Azw3 formats.

To get set up for this conversion, we'll load a free app called Calibre.

Free App Installation for Calibre

1. Go to http://calibre-ebook.com.

2. Select the **Download Calibre** button.

3. Pick your operating system or OS.

4. Select the **Download Calibre** link.

5. After it downloads, install it on your computer.

 The Calibre manual is located at https://manual.calibre-ebook.com.

Conversion to Mobi using Calibre

1. Open the Calibre app.

2. Select **Add Books** and point Calibre to the folder with your epub book file. Calibre imports the ebook and lists your book as the top book on the list.

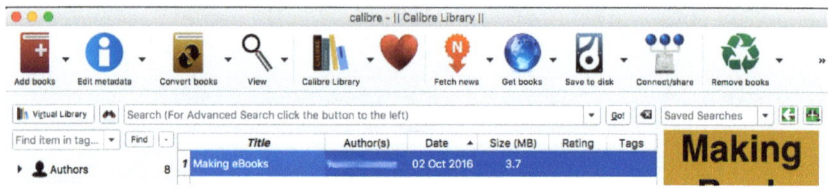

Figure 24. The ePub book loaded into Calibre

3. Select the book you want to convert to Mobi format for Amazon reader devices.

4. Select **Convert Books**. The convert window opens.

5. If you want the Mobi format, select **mobi** as the output format as shown.

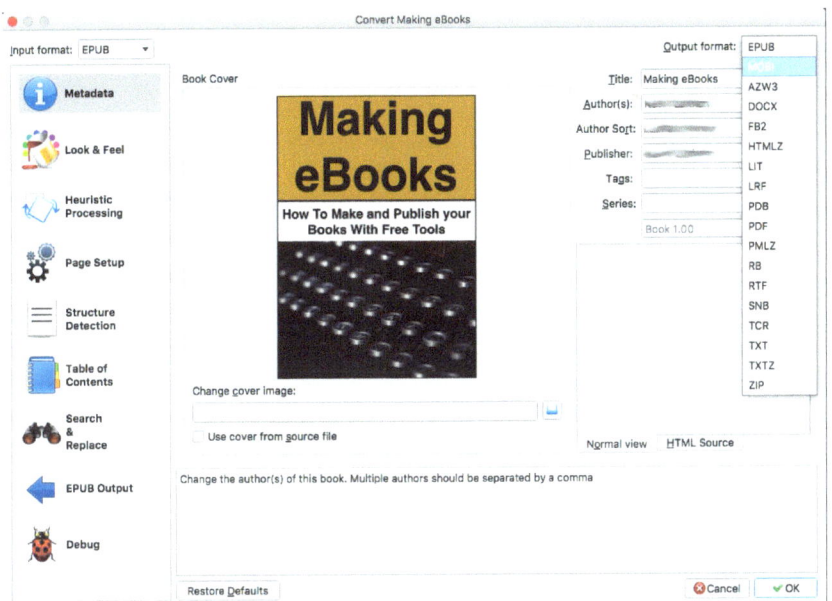

Figure 25. Picking the Mobi Output Format

6. If you want the newer Amazon AZW3 format, select **AZW3** as the output format as shown.

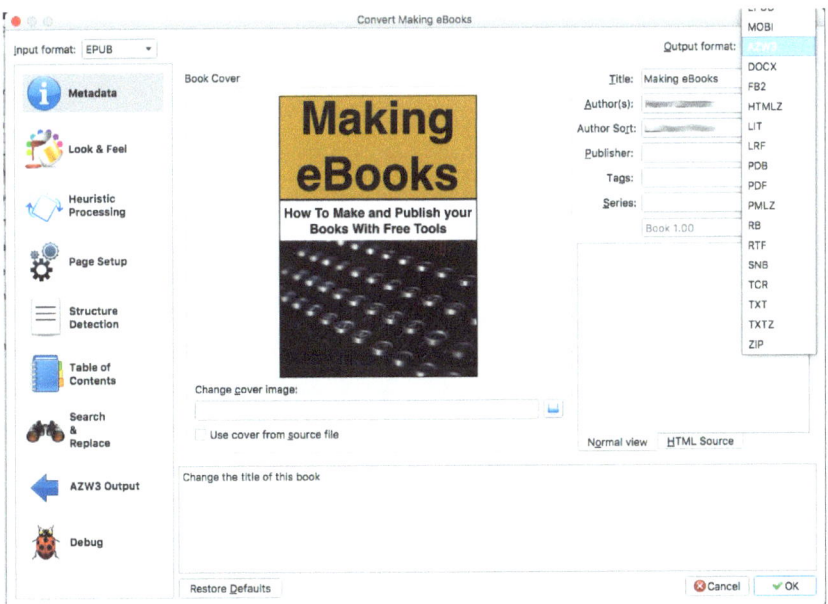

Figure 26. Picking the AZW3 Output Format

7. After Calibre shows the conversion job is done, select the book in Calibre and select **Save to Disk**.

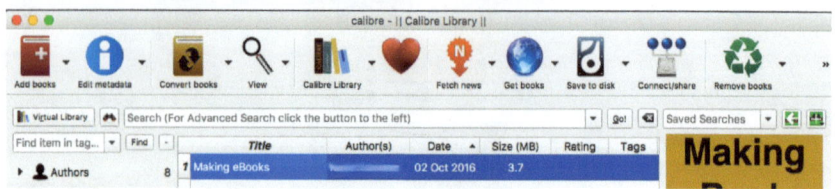

Figure 27. Saving the Converted Book

8. Find the *.mobi or *.azw3 format eBook on your computer drive.

9. Quit the Calibre app.

Another way to convert ePub to amazon format is to use the free Amazon command line app called KindleGen. [16: To download KindelGen, see URL www.amazon.com/kindleformat/kindlegen] At the time of publishing, Amazon even created a manual for how to do it. [17: See Amazon's manual at URL http://kindlegen.s3.amazonaws.com/AmazonKindlePublishingGuidelines.pdf]

How to Test your eBook on Your Reader

We want to test our eBook before we send it out to the world. It's better when we catch mistakes before our audience finds them. We won't be perfect, but we want to seek as much perfection as we can in our process for producing a book for the world.

So how do we do this? I offer a way. You may find other ways you like better. The point is be sure to test that your eBook works before you distribute it.

If you have a mobile device like a phone, you can load a reader app. If you use the Android OS, load the Adobe Digital Editions app. If you use iOS, then a reader app is pre-installed. It is called iBooks. If you have no mobile device, but have a computer you can also load the Adobe Digital Editions app.

One Way to Test a eBook

1. Check that your device has an eReader app installed. If not, find one you like and install it. If you want one that works across platforms (Windows, MacOS, Linux) load the Adobe Digital Editions app.

2. Make your eBook. Use the instructions in the rest of this book to make your eBook.

3. Once you have your ePub file, in my example my file "Making_eBooks.epub" is the eBook version of this book.

4. Get the eBook to your **iOS device**.

   a. Email the *.epub file to yourself as an attachment.

   b. Open the mail with your iOS device.

   c. Click the *.epub attachment.

   d. The iOS device will ask if you want to open it with iBooks. Select iBooks.

5. Get the eBook to your **Android device**.

   a. If your device has a removable SD or microSD card, copy the file onto that card and insert the card into the device.

   b. Download and install FBReader on your Android device. You can get the FBReader reader app from Google Play. [18:   See https://play.google.com/store/apps/details?id=org.geometerplus.zlibrary.ui.android]

   c. On the Android device, open the FBreader app.

d. Select **File Tree | Memory Card** and navigate to the location of the *.epub file.

e. Select the book to view the metadata.

f. Select the **Read** button to open the book.

g. This is only one method. Use your favorite reader to check your book if you prefer. Other readers include Aldiko Book Reader, Adobe Digital Editions, and many other readers on Google Play.

6. Get the eBook to your **Amazon Kindle device**.

a. Open your computer folder with the *.AZW3 or *.mobi file.

b. Plug your kindle into your computer with the USB charging cable. The Kindle device opens like another drive folder.

c. Drag and drop your *.AZW3 or *.mobi file from your computer folder to the Kindle folder.

d. Eject and disconnect your Kindle from the computer.

e. Remove the USB charging cable from the Kindle.

f. Open the Kindle and go to your library.

g. You should see your eBook listed as one of the books available.

7. Review the eBook on the device eReader app.

a. Check that all your images came through the publishing process.

b. Check that the table of contents works.

c. Check that the cover shows up correctly.

d. Make sure your eBook is formatted so that it is readable.

Another way to get an eBook to your Reader and to your reviewer's readers is to put the eBook on Dropbox and send the URL to yourself and your reviewers. Once you go to the Dropbox URL, the rest of the steps are just like after the email is opened.

I use the flowable eBook formatting meaning that the content flows onto the screen differently depending on the device screen size. For people used to fixed layout, there is a another format just for fixed layout but I don't care to mess with that layout. People that produce magazines may. If you really want to try for fixed layout on readers that can't even reliably produce tables yet, have at it. As for me, I am satisfied with the flowable eBook layout.

A To Do List Inside the Book Draft

Sometimes it helps to have a to do list for seeing visual progress in a writing project. You may have a favorite way of tracking to do items for your book, but if not, consider tracking to dos for your book inside the book draft.

AsciiDoc lets you create to do lists directly in your book draft so you know where your to do list is located. This can be especially helpful if you only write part-time with many hours or days between writing sessions. The to do list also helps you build your book incrementally, little by little, line by line.

 Remember to remove or comment out all to do list items before publishing your book. These lists are for the author, not for the reader.

Backlog

- ☐ Add images 📷
- ☐ Add index entries
- ☐ Check that all images are sized correctly for the paper size 6x9
- ☐ Add install instructions for each of the free tools

Work In Progress (WIP) - Research

None

WIP - Create Content

☐ How? Content

WIP - Testing Functionality & Content Checking (Edits, Style, etc.)

☐ Why? Content

Done

☑ Mindmap Content Structure

☑ Test epub publishing using minimal content

☑ Test conditional publishing for print vs HTML5 using minimal content

The Secret to Nearly Free Reviews

This chapter alone is worth more than the price you paid for this book.

This chapter describes a way to review that is not strictly free, but is relatively low cost.

Some people suggest reading the draft out loud. This can work. It also takes much time to do.

Creating a voice audio of the entire draft takes only seconds using the audio review method. Save all that other time for the other great parts of life. I listen to my book to edit for mistakes and problems. This works very well for me. It helps me hear someone else's voice reading my manuscript or book draft, which makes me a bit more critical of what I'm hearing to better catch parts that sound funny or odd. Digital audio is easy to playback and listen again to confirm there's an issue with the writing. My writing problems happen much more often than the automated voice pronouncing something wrong.

Automated voice, or text to speech apps, are getting much better. However, they almost always mangle the pronunciation of a particular word. Then I can decide whether I care to fix the pronunciation configuration of the text to speech app so it pronounces the word better, or decide if you'll just work around it (my vote). Remember the product is a written book, not an audio book. The automated voice is to help you review with your hearing, not to be good enough to sell as an audio book. By the way, if you figure that out, please write your own book so I can learn from you.

In my past commercial use of automated voice, or text to speech apps, I have spent much time configuring the robot voice to sound more human. In my opinion, given the purpose of review, it is not worth all the time you'll spend configuring. If you decide to make an audio book, hire a human voice actor to read your book. I can ignore the mispronunciation for the brief period of review.

The benefits of this approach for me include:

- **Convert dead time** formerly used only to commute **into productive editing time**

- Use **your ears to catch issues** that your eyes glossed right over

- I set the app to **speed up the pace of the recorded audio** to faster than humans typically speak to help me review more content in less time. I don't go to the point where the audio sounds like chipmunks, but it is faster than the normal 120 words per minute we hear in conversation.

I use a small collection of tools to review by ear.

- Text to Voice app that exports to MP3 format

- MP3 Player (mine is built into my car stereo) with **easy stop and start controls** you can feel without looking to aid safe driving

- Digital recorder to note changes that need to be made after my commute

All Text to Voice apps currently have a strange accent. I have found that Australian female voices tend to be the least difficult to listen to. You don't really care about the accent if you can understand it. The goal is for your ear to catch oddities in your writing. Even with the strange accent, the Text to Voice app will faithfully say exactly what you typed. If it sounds off, then you likely made a mistake in writing. The ear catches mistakes that the eye misses after it has gone over the draft a few times.

Even if you don't have an MP3 player in your vehicle, you can record MP3 format to a plastic CDROM and play it on older handheld CD players. Use the technologies available to help you speed your work.

Here is how I do it.

1. I use AsciiDoctor to publish the draft to HTML.

2. I copy all of the HTML page from the browser and paste it into the Text-to-Voice app.

3. I export the draft book as a voice recording by an automated voice to MP3 format.

4. I put the MP3 file on my car player and begin the drive to work.

5. I keep my digital recorder close at hand so I can stop the MP3 book recording and make a voice note of what my ears heard that was weird or off.

6. I stop the car MP3 player by pressing one physical button.

7. I turn on the digital recorder with one button (the Sony

record button is concave so I can feel the right button without looking away from traffic).

8. I say to the digital recorder "Look for the phrase 'the dog jumped over the moon' (or whatever phrase was just before the error my ears caught) and then I explain what was wrong and how to fix it.

9. I press the stop button on the digital recorder.

10. I press the start button on the car MP3 player.

11. I repeat the process while in routine traffic situations.

 Do not attempt this in complex traffic situations. Be safe first. Be a writer second.

12. I make review voice annotations during my drive to work.

13. I make review voice annotations during my drive home.

14. At home, I open the HTML version of the entire book and search for the phrase I caught near the error.

15. I then back up to the nearest chapter or section heading, so I know which file to open to edit the error. This is because my file names match my section headings or chapter titles.

16. I locate the location phrase 'the dog jumped over the moon' with the find function.

17. I see the error I heard and make the fix I recorded.

18. I save the file.

19. The next day I make another HTML draft version, a new MP3 file, and repeat the process.

Because these drafts are digital, I'm not wasting paper with paper edits as frequently.

To get kitted up for this method do the following.

Buy an inexpensive digital recorder with appropriate features:

- Easy-to-use button controls with no log-in required (like on a mobile phone) or other delays

- Press record, talk, press stop

- Look for the least features to keep it easy to use

- Look for sales, but prioritize ease-of-use button controls over saving $10.

 Pay attention to the ease of controls. I use this while driving, so I can feel the record button without looking down. Easy controls also reduce the transaction waste each time I have to turn the recorder on and off.

 I do NOT use my mobile phone to do this recording. The mobile phone's required security log-in adds too much delay for me. You may want to if you're at home or in your office and can tolerate the delay. But I use this while driving, so I prioritized for ease-of-use for safety due to minimal cognitive loading to the driver.

Sony ICD-BX132 Digital Voice Recorder
by Sony
★★★★☆ ▾   40 customer reviews | 10 answered questions

Price: $45.99 & **FREE Shipping** on orders over $49. Details

Only 1 left in stock.
Want it Wednesday, Sept. 21? Order within **2 hrs 49 mins** and choose **Two-Day Shipping** at checkout. Details
Sold by Bedding and Beyond and Fulfilled by Amazon. Gift-wrap available.

• Sony 2GB Memory Digital Voice Recorder

7 new from $35.00   3 used from $24.95   3 refurbished from $19.70

▢ Report incorrect product information.

Roll over image to zoom in

Figure 28. The Sony Similar to What I Use

For the Mac I use the Text2Speech Pro app, for which I paid $3.99 US Dollars.

For Windows I've used NextUp's TextAloud (see http://nextup.com/purchase.html) which was about $30 as I recall.

The car I'm using has a stereo that plays MP3, so that is already part of my infrastructure for audible review of my book drafts.

For example, in two 40-minute drives to and from work I found about 40 issues in the audio version of my book first draft. I made notes on my digital recorder. I have one digital recording per issue. Then I was able to go back and fix those issues during the evenings and weekends so readers don't have to encounter those issues. This gives my book higher quality than it would if I relied entirely on visual editing.

I strongly recommend this audio review method.

Conditional Publishing

 This is an advanced topic. If you are new to AsciiDoc you should skip this chapter until you have practiced and gotten better at AsciiDoc. I don't recommend this to new people.

 This is the feature of Asciidoc that I use to switch between the 72 dpi images for eBooks and the 300 dpi images for print books.

When you use AsciiDoctor as the rendering app for AsciiDoc content you can render the content in a conditional way.

Why would you want to publish based on a condition, you might ask. As an example, I wrote a genealogy book that had details I wanted to share with family, but not with the general public. So I made one condition "public" which only showed information about people who have already died. The other condition was "living" which surrounded personal information like date of birth, and other details we don't want floating around in public.

AsciiDoctor has a way to facilitate conditional publishing, or as Dan Allen calls it, conditional pre-processing.

To use conditional publishing we first set a flag of sorts in the book attributes by inventing our own special conditional code. For example in my genealogy book, the flags or attributes were "living" and "public". In another book, I might want to use "eBook" and "printPDF" to identify sections of content. You may makeup whatever codes you like to flag AsciiDoctor. The key thing is to add your flag as an attribute in the front of your book.

Do not add a blank line between your conditional attribute and the other book attributes or it may not work.

Next we surround the content we want conditional with a small set of codes that tell AsciiDoctor to check the attribute before rendering this part.

For example, a paragraph in a chapter or section might have a table which only works well in PDF, not eBooks. So I would add the conditional codes around the table for "printPDF" and have a bulleted form of the content wrapped with "eBook" conditional flag. The only one to show up would be the one with the attribute set at the front of the book.

```
= Example Conditional Publishing Book
:author: Michael Lynnmore
:printPDF: ①

This paragraph shows up in all conditions. ②

ifdef::printPDF[] ③
This portion was made for PDF to facilitate printing.
Perhaps this section has a table that only renders well
in PDF format. ④
endif::[] ⑤

ifdef::eBook[] ⑥
This portion was made for eBooks. ⑦
A bulleted list might replace the table in this section.
endif::[] ⑧
```

① The printPDF is the attribute that flags AsciiDoctor to render all the common content and the content marked by this attribute.

② This paragraph is an example of common content which will render for all conditions.

③ This is the beginning code for the condition "printPDF".

④ This is the "printPDF" conditional content.

⑤ This is the ending code for the conditional "printPDF".

⑥ This is the beginning code for the condition "eBook".

⑦ This is the "eBook" conditional content.

⑧ This is the ending code for the conditional "eBook".

Using Version Control

This is an advanced topic. If you are new to AsciiDoc you should skip this chapter until you have practiced and gotten better at AsciiDoc.

If you decide not to use version control, you can also gain a backup by using Dropbox. Because your AsciiDoc files are plain text, they take up very little space. If you lose your computer and have to start over, you can go to Dropbox and synch your files and be on your way with little disruption.

Version control apps record changes to your book files over time so that you can go back to to earlier versions if needed. These apps let you easily store versions of your work as it changes.

Version control can work on images too.

For me the biggest feature about version control is the ability to **compare changes over time** from version A to version B to let me see what has changed in my book over time as I write it.

Because most version control apps were designed to tracking code, which has one commands per line, the version differences are tracked one line at a time in your book AsciiDoc plain text.

Dan Allen, the person who brought us the AsciiDoctor app, recommends that we write one sentence per line in the text editor, Atom (or your favorite), so the version control app can show how each sentence changed over time.

To do this, I set up my asciidoctor to combine each line into a paragraph. When I need a paragraph break, I add a blank line between two sentences.

Dan's idea works fantastically and has helped me improve my writing as I input changes from reviewers and editors.

Version control tracks your complete change history over the life of your book project. This can help you see how your project evolved. It can also potentially help with copyright infringement legal proceedings because it can provide proof that you wrote the book.

If you're collaborating with others to write a book, you can share version control like git (more on that later) and see who made a change that introduced a problem.

The free version control app I recommend is called git.

You can get it at https://git-scm.com.

Look for the downloads page at https://git-scm.com/downloads.

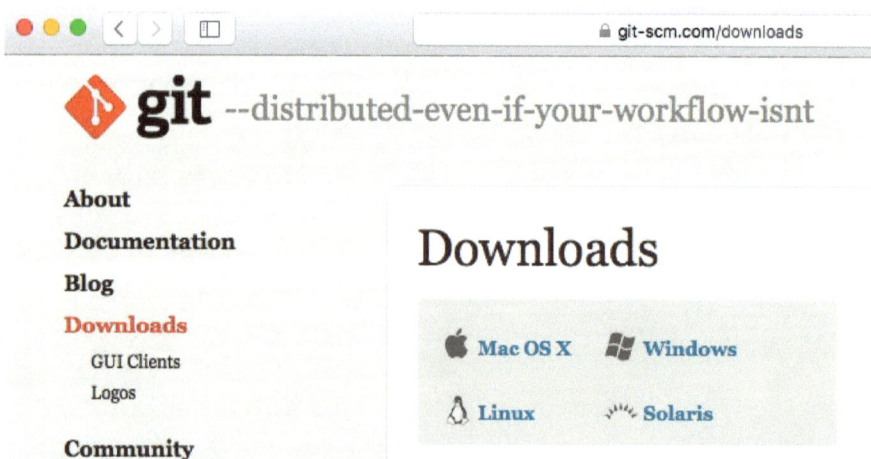

Figure 29. Git Downloads Include All Platforms

How to Get your Print Book Published in Paper

 There is no way to print a book for free. You can publish an eBook (bits) free if you don't count your own labor. But to go to print requires paper and toner or ink, a binding to hold the pages together, and shipping costs to mail the heavy book (atoms) somewhere.

One method is to go to https://www.createspace.com and follow their guidelines. This is not a free option, but going from bits to atoms will cost money because of the consumables used in the printing process.

Another site that helps is http://www.blurb.com. Again, not free.

 You will need to create two (2) of every image you add to a printed book. One for the eBook and one for the printed book. This is because resolution on screen is about 72 dpi, while on paper it is about 300 dpi. This dots per inch (dpi) resolution will make 72 dpi fuzzy if printed and 300 dpi enormous if used as the screen version. So you'll need to swap out the images depending on the target output format to keep the resolution appropriate.

Show Your Customers How To Use Readers

You might want to go all digital. You might want to avoid print books to save trees and prevent more waste in landfills.

Yet, I have run into many people who still do not know how to use eBooks yet.

- How to get the *.epub file on their device
- How to use the reader app to read the eBook

I have had to teach them how to use:

- iBooks reader app (iOS, MacOS)
- Adobe Digital Editions reader app (iOS, Android OS, Windows OS)
- Amazon handheld readers with e-ink

Tips and Tricks

Here are lessons I learned the hard way so you don't have to.

Titles

For a book title that has a sub title, use a colon to separate the title from the subtitle. For example in this book, it includes a subtitle and it is separated by a colon. I tried a hyphen first and that didn't work. Colon is the right separator for AsciiDoctor.

```
= AsciiDoc Authoring: How To Make Books For Free ①
```

① Note the ':' colon character as the separator.

One Sentence Per Line

Dan Allen recommended this and I think it has worked really well for me. It really shines when you use version control app to show the differences between versions over time.

The asciidoctor app puts all the sentences back into paragraphs for the published or rendered versions.

Image Borders

To automatically add a border around an image, add the following around it.

```
[.thumb] ①
.The Sony Similar to What I Use ②
image::media\DigitalRecorder.png[] ③
```

① This AsciiDoctor code adds the border around the image.

② This is the figure title.

③ This is the image path and filename reference.

Fonts

Add the following attribute to the book file as follows.

```
= AsciiDoc Authoring: How To Make Books For Free
:author: Michael Lynnmore
:icons: font ①
```

① The icons attribute with the word font to the right turns on the fonts for callouts and admonitions. Do not leave a blank line between the attributes and the title.

Comments for intellectual property notes

Use comments for IP notes.

For example, for an image I got from a open licensing source, I can include the license type and the URL in a comment.

Comments for AsciiDoc are two forward slashes //.

Here is an example for attribution of an image.

```
.My Sample Image
image::media\MickeyMouseImage.png[]
// Pending permission from Disney. Request sent on 2016-
07-15.
```

This keeps the IP to dos in proximity to the usage. When I get permission then I use a footnote to provide attribution rather than break the content.

Comments for Work to Be Done Later

I sometimes use comments to remind myself of the idea at a high level using comments. For example, consider this example source text in AsciiDoc.

```
Here is a paragraph, blah blah blah.

// Add a summary of the Huckleberry Finn story

Here is another paragraph, yada yada yada.
```

The nice thing about comments is that they don't render to the reader's version. They're just for the creators.

Gotchas

This chapter shares some of the stumbling I had when I initially learned how to use AsciiDoc. I share it to help you avoid the same mistakes.

Image Issues

It took me a while to realize I was being sloppy and causing my own problems. For example images are called by AsciiDoc using the delineator image::.

images::media\filename.png[] will **not** work

image::media\filename.png[] **will** work

It took me ten minutes to find the issue. Hopefully you can learn from my mistake and avoid this problem. The delineator is image::, not images::. There is no 's' in the delineator.

Here's an example of what you'll see when you do it wrong. The AsciiDoc code shows up in the book. This is an actual example of my own mistake while making this book.

9. Use AsciiDoctor to render the prototype file to HTML or PDF.

   a. Use the rendering instructions elsewhere in this book.

   b. My prototype folder looks like this when done.

   Prototype Files in my Folder
   images::media\PrototypeFiles.png[]

10. Show the result to a potential member of your intended audience

Figure 30. Wrong Way Shows Code Instead of the Image

Compare that to how it looks when done correctly.

9. Use AsciiDoctor to render the prototype file to HTML or PDF.

    a. Use the rendering instructions elsewhere in this book.

    b. My prototype folder looks like this when done.

    m Book Prototype.mm
       Prototype.adoc
    • Prototype.html
    ⌐ Prototype.pdf

Figure 3. Prototype Files in my Folder

10. Show the result to a potential member of your intended audience

Figure 31. Correct Way Shows the Image

Another way to break images in AsciiDoc is to leave off the square brackets at the end of the image reference. The rendering app will give you an error for this mistake too.

 Be careful until you build good AsciiDoc habits.

Another image problem is using rastor images not sized for your output. I edit their size with the Gimp app.

Tables Don't Work Well Yet in Most eReaders

When I write technical documents and nonfiction, I am used to using tables. Simple tables to complex tables help communicate. I got tables working great on the first big book (80,000 words) I wrote and I tested to PDF regularly. However, when I got to eBooks the tables came out so poorly that I had to convert them to bulleted lists instead. I tried tables on Kindle e-ink readers, iBooks on iOS phones and iPads, and Adobe's Digital Editions. They were not acceptable quality. As the reader, I was not happy with the output of tables to any of these eBook readers.

So you don't have to experience the table pain I did, you can:

- **Option A**: Avoid tables altogether. Switch from tabular structure to a bulleted list structure.
- **Option B**: Use conditional publishing with AsciiDoctor and render tables for PDF and bullet lists for smaller eReader screens.

As eReader technology improves, perhaps tables will render better in eBook formats. If you think about it, the large majority of eBooks today are fiction novels that are largely narrative text. So eReader apps were optimized for large areas of text.

 If you plan to use tables, see AsciiDoc Reference for sites that show how to use tables in AsciiDoc. I'm not going to cover tables because so few reader apps today render them well. If you do decide to use tables, you may want to use conditional publishing and use tables in PDFs for print and bullet lists of the same content for most eReaders. See Conditional Publishing for details on conditional publishing.

If You're Going to Use Conditional Publishing, Change your Attribute Flags

This may sound obvious, but when I got into a deadline crunch I published a conditional publishing book to both conditions, but I forgot to set the conditional attribute flags for the situation.

It is not too big of a problem. It just involves a small amount of rework in the automated production. To HTML, you won't notice the change. For a large book going to PDF, it means waiting minutes. It is not too long, but is about as much fun as waiting for an elevator to come to your floor.

Footnote Problems

Early in my use of AsciiDoc I had issues with footnotes because **I forgot** the include the **colon**. Notice that in the example, the colon is after the "footnote" key word and before the square brackets [].

```
footnote:[Here is the text of the footnote that will show
up at the bottom of the page for PDF or at the end of the
book for HTML.]
```

If you forget and drop the colon, it can be self-correcting because you'll see no linked number and no footnote with that reference number. Instead you'll see the inline footnote AsciiDoc code instead.

Here is a correct footnote **example.** [19: An example footnote only]

Here is an incorrect footnote example.footnote[An example footnote only]

See how the two contrasting examples render differently? The correct example renders to an inline number that links to the footnote at the bottom of the page (PDF) or end of the book (HTML).

So when you render to HTML or PDF and you see any AsciiDoc codes still showing that tells you a mistake was made (notice the passive voice?). Yes, that tells you that you made a mistake and need to go back and add the colon.

When using audio review (see The Secret to Nearly Free Reviews), if you hear the word footnote in an unusual place, that's your cue that you missed the colon too. If you hear a number at the end of a sentence while listening to the audio version of the book draft, that means it rendered correctly.

The good news is that it's not a difficult fix. The rendering app does what it's told to do. So when it doesn't look as expected, that's your cue.

Having Internet Access During Rendering

If you use the attribute **:icons: font**, this needs access to the internet to work when you render to HTML. I had turned off my wireless for a while, and when I came back to the book draft none of the icons for admonitions were working.

After some troubleshooting, I realized the only thing that had changed was my shutting off the internet access. So I tested it with the internet on again (wireless on), rendered to HTML and it worked fine.

Conclusion

Today, we have all these wonderful free or low cost tools to create, be more productive, and improve our quality.

By using this combination of tools, I've been able to see a dramatic increase in productivity.

You still have to come with the idea and do the work of writing. And the technology helps save a lot of time on the tedious portions involved in taking our draft to a final published version ready for distribution. Most of us don't like the tedious portions anyway.

The time these tools save make it worthwhile to learn how to use plain text and AsciiDoc in particular.

AsciiDoc Reference

Here are some of the best reference sites for learning new AsciiDoc I did not cover or to remember things if you're online.

- AsciiDoc User Guide (http://www.methods.co.nz/asciidoc/userguide.html)

- Asciidoctor User Manual (http://asciidoctor.org/docs/user-manual/)

- AsciiDoc cheatsheet by Powerman (https://powerman.name/doc/asciidoc)

- Awesome Asciidoctor Notebook (https://leanpub.com/awesomeasciidoctornotebook/read)

Some Source AsciiDoc For This Book

Sometimes it helps to see what someone else has done. So here is the AsciiDoc that I used for this book so you can see how I did it.

I personally tend towards modular documents, so here is my book skeleton with conditional flags set to PDF.

```
= Making eBooks: How To Make and Publish your Books With
Free Tools
:author: by Michael Lynnmore
:icons: font
:doctype: book
:asciidoctor:
:toc:
:toclevels: 1
// We don't add the toc when going to eBooks because the
other application will generate the TOC instead.
:pdf-page-size: [6in, 9in]
:PDFoutput:
// This flag has to be turned on for PDF resolution
images to show up correctly.

//:HTMLoutput:
// This flag has to be turned on for HTML resolution
images to render for ebooks and html pages.

include::Chapters_and_Sections/Copyright.adoc[]

include::Chapters_and_Sections/Introduction.adoc[]

include::Chapters_and_Sections/Preface.adoc[]
```

```
include::Chapters_and_Sections/Acknowledgements.adoc[]

include::Chapters_and_Sections/Conventions.adoc[]

include::Chapters_and_Sections/WhyPlainText.adoc[]

include::Chapters_and_Sections/WhyDIY.adoc[]

include::Chapters_and_Sections/ByExample.adoc[]

include::Chapters_and_Sections/AuthoringSetUp.adoc[]

include::Chapters_and_Sections/Prototyping.adoc[]

include::Chapters_and_Sections/UsingFreeMindMappingTool.a
doc[]

include::Chapters_and_Sections/UsingTheCommandLine.adoc[]

include::Chapters_and_Sections/FirstAttemptAuthoring.adoc
[]

include::Chapters_and_Sections/RenderingSetUp.adoc[]

include::Chapters_and_Sections/FirstAttemptRendering.adoc
[]

include::Chapters_and_Sections/LetsAddImages.adoc[]

include::Chapters_and_Sections/LetsAddaCrossReference.ado
c[]

include::Chapters_and_Sections/LetsAddFootnotes.adoc[]

include::Chapters_and_Sections/LetsAddIndexEntriesForPrin
t.adoc[]

include::Chapters_and_Sections/LetsAddGlossaryTerms.adoc[
```

```
]

include::Chapters_and_Sections/ABookSkeleton.adoc[]

include::Chapters_and_Sections/MakeAPDFforPrint.adoc[]

include::Chapters_and_Sections/MakeAnEBook.adoc[]

include::Chapters_and_Sections/ToDoListsInTheBook.adoc[]

include::Chapters_and_Sections/TheSecretToNearlyFreeRevie
ws.adoc[]

include::Chapters_and_Sections/ConditionalPublishing.adoc
[]

include::Chapters_and_Sections/UsingVersionControl.adoc[]

include::Chapters_and_Sections/HowToGetPrintBookPublished
.adoc[]

include::Chapters_and_Sections/ShowCustomersHowToUseReade
rs.adoc[]

include::Chapters_and_Sections/TipsAndTricks.adoc[]

include::Chapters_and_Sections/Gotchas.adoc[]

include::Chapters_and_Sections/Conclusion.adoc[]

include::Chapters_and_Sections/AsciiDocReference.adoc[]

include::Chapters_and_Sections/SourceForThisBook.adoc[]

include::Chapters_and_Sections/colophon.adoc[]

include::glossaryTerms\Glossary_Intro.adoc[]
```

```
== Thank You
Thank you for purchasing this book.
Please write a review on the site you purchased it.
```

Here is a simple portion to see how I wrote the AsciiDoc for the introduction of this book.

Notice how I use the one sentence per line. It renders as a paragraph, but having one sentence per line helps the version control system show me how the sentence has changed as I edit.

```
== Introduction
What if you could control the entire process of writing
your book, production and distribution using free tools?
You can.
This book shows you how to do that.
This book assumes you have a computer and access to the
internet.

Sure, you can pay other people to convert your content
into an eBook for you, each time you need a conversion.
If that's your plan, you do not need this book.
If you'd rather easily do it yourself for free, as many
times as you'd like, then this book is for you.

NOTE: You don't need to get this book to figure this out.
You can figure it out for yourself if you'd like. This
book simply helps people learn from what I learned while
I figured it out.

Making eBooks is still a process in its infancy as our
society transitions from paper publishing to electronic
publishing.
Nicolas Negroponte discussed the differences between bits
and atoms in his 1995 book __Being Digital__. Twenty one
years later, we're just starting to achieve momentum with
digital publishing as more eBooks are sold than paper
```

books.
Atoms make up the physical objects in our world such as
plastic DVDs, CDs, and paper books.
Digital information, like eBooks, are made up of bits,
the smallest unit of information on a computer.
The tools have advanced for publishing digital or
electronic books, sometimes called eBooks.

The process is sure to change as tools continue to
improve.

Creating this book was fun. Just making the book made it
a successful project for me.
I enjoyed making it.
Perhaps you will enjoy making your own eBooks and print
books this way too.

The journey to discover how and **the challenge** of
getting it right **drew me in**.
After much trial and error, when **I finally got it all
working** I felt like jumping in the air and shouting
Eureka!

This book also **extends my own memory** of how I made
and published eBooks and print books.
I wrote this book because if life takes me on a different
path for too long and I forget how I did it, then this
book is my own "how to" instructions **to my future
self** when I need to write and publish again.
Potentially other people may see the value of this book
too.

One last point.
There exist some excellent online tools that I don't show
in this book because I don't want them to disappear
during a project if they run out of startup money and go
out of business.
The tools I chose to use and explain in this book are

```
downloadable.
This lets you have control of your project's
infrastructure.
You may want to use those online tools.
I'm only showing how to use the ones you can download.
```

If your head is already full, then stop here. However, if you want to see conditional publishing at work, read on.

If you're ready, here is a big chunk of a more complex chapter of this book so you can see how I use conditionals for eBooks or print books.

The ". blah blah" format is for ordered lists. The "+" sign helps keep the numbered items together so when it renders it keeps #4 after #3, for example.

```
=== Make EPUB Format eBook for all Readers Except Kindle

. Open the Sigil app on your computer.
+
ifdef::HTMLoutput[]
.Opening Screen for Sigil
image::media\SigilOpenScreen.png[]
endif::HTMLoutput[]

ifdef::PDFoutput[]
.Opening Screen for Sigil
image::media\SigilOpenScreen_300dpi.png[]
endif::PDFoutput[]
+
. Ignore most of what you see.
. Select the Text folder as shown.
+
ifdef::HTMLoutput[]
image::media\Sigil1.png[]
endif::HTMLoutput[]
```

```
ifdef::PDFoutput[]
image::media\Sigil1_300dpi.png[]
endif::PDFoutput[]
+
. Select **File | Add | Existing Files** as shown.
+
ifdef::HTMLoutput[]
image::media\SigilAddExistingFile.png[]
endif::HTMLoutput[]

ifdef::PDFoutput[]
image::media\SigilAddExistingFile_300dpi.png[]
endif::PDFoutput[]
+
. Navigate to your working folder where you have the book
files and select the book file HTML version, for my book
is MakeBooksFree.html. This screenshot shows using the
add existing file icon rather than the file menus.
+
ifdef::HTMLoutput[]
image::media\SigilAddExistingFileNext.png[]
endif::HTMLoutput[]

ifdef::PDFoutput[]
image::media\SigilAddExistingFileNext_300dpi.png[]
endif::PDFoutput[]
+
. Check that your book file was added. See in the example
how MakeBooksFree.html now shows up.
+
ifdef::HTMLoutput[]
image::media\SigilAddedMyHTMLBookFile.png[]
endif::HTMLoutput[]

ifdef::PDFoutput[]
image::media\SigilAddedMyHTMLBookFile_300dpi.png[]
endif::PDFoutput[]
```

+
. Select the default file that was included in Sigil,
called Section0001.xhtml, and press your delete key. The
__Delete Files__ window pops up with the
Section0001.xhtml file checked.
+
ifdef::HTMLoutput[]
image::media\SigilDeleteDefaultFile.png[]
endif::HTMLoutput[]

ifdef::PDFoutput[]
image::media\SigilDeleteDefaultFile_300dpi.png[]
endif::PDFoutput[]
+
. Confirm Section0001.xhtml shows in the delete window
and select **Delete Marked Files** button at the bottom
of the __Delete Files__ window.
+
ifdef::HTMLoutput[]
image::media\SigilDeleteFilesWindow.png[]
endif::HTMLoutput[]

ifdef::PDFoutput[]
image::media\SigilDeleteFilesWindow_300dpi.png[]
endif::PDFoutput[]
+
. The default file should disappear, leaving only your
book file.
+
ifdef::HTMLoutput[]
image::media\SigilYourBookShowsUp.png[]
endif::HTMLoutput[]

ifdef::PDFoutput[]
image::media\SigilYourBookShowsUp_300dpi.png[]
endif::PDFoutput[]
+
. Select **Tools | Table of Contents | Generate Table of

Contents**
+
ifdef::HTMLoutput[]
image::media\SigilGenerateTOC.png[]
endif::HTMLoutput[]

ifdef::PDFoutput[]
image::media\SigilGenerateTOC_300dpi.png[]
endif::PDFoutput[]
+
. Select the titles you don't want in the Table of
Contents and they disappear. In my screenshot example,
I'm removing all the h3 titles so my TOC is not too
cluttered.
+
ifdef::HTMLoutput[]
image::media\SigilTOCSelector.png[]
endif::HTMLoutput[]

ifdef::PDFoutput[]
image::media\SigilTOCSelector_300dpi.png[]
endif::PDFoutput[]
+
. Select the **OK** button and the eBook table of
contents is automatically generated.
+
ifdef::HTMLoutput[]
image::media\SigilTOCGenerated.png[]
endif::HTMLoutput[]

ifdef::PDFoutput[]
image::media\SigilTOCGenerated_300dpi.png[]
endif::PDFoutput[]
+
. Select **Tools | Add Cover**.
+
ifdef::HTMLoutput[]
image::media\SigilAddCoverMenu.png[]

```
endif::HTMLoutput[]

ifdef::PDFoutput[]
image::media\SigilAddCoverMenu_300dpi.png[]
endif::PDFoutput[]
+
. The cover image selector window opens. Select your
cover graphic file and select **OK**.
+
ifdef::HTMLoutput[]
image::media\SigilCoverImportWindow.png[]
endif::HTMLoutput[]

ifdef::PDFoutput[]
image::media\SigilCoverImportWindow_300dpi.png[]
endif::PDFoutput[]
+
. Your cover should show up as a new tab in the middle
pane of Sigil as shown.
+
ifdef::HTMLoutput[]
image::media\SigilCoverAttached.png[]
endif::HTMLoutput[]

ifdef::PDFoutput[]
image::media\SigilCoverAttached_300dpi.png[]
endif::PDFoutput[]
+
. Select **Tools | Well Formed Check EPUB** to validate
your eBook.
+
ifdef::HTMLoutput[]
image::media\SigilWellFormedCheck.png[]
endif::HTMLoutput[]

ifdef::PDFoutput[]
image::media\SigilWellFormedCheck_300dpi.png[]
endif::PDFoutput[]
```

+
. Check that the validation results pane message shows
"No problems found."
. Select **Tools | Metadata Editor** to add metadata to
your eBook.
+
ifdef::HTMLoutput[]
image::media\SigilMetaDataWindow1.png[]
endif::HTMLoutput[]

ifdef::PDFoutput[]
image::media\SigilMetaDataWindow1_300dpi.png[]
endif::PDFoutput[]
+
. Select **Add Metadata** and select the metadata type
you want to add. For example, Author.
. Click on the field that shows **[No Data]**, and type
in what you want instead.
. When done adding metadata select the **OK** button.
+
ifdef::HTMLoutput[]
image::media\SigilMetaDataWindow2.png[]
endif::HTMLoutput[]

ifdef::PDFoutput[]
image::media\SigilMetaDataWindow2_300dpi.png[]
endif::PDFoutput[]
+
. Select **File | Save As**.
+
ifdef::HTMLoutput[]
image::media\SigilFileSaveAs.png[]
endif::HTMLoutput[]

ifdef::PDFoutput[]
image::media\SigilFileSaveAs_300dpi.png[]
endif::PDFoutput[]
+

. Add the filename for your eBook then select **Save**.
+
ifdef::HTMLoutput[]
image::media\SigilNameeBookFile.png[]
endif::HTMLoutput[]

ifdef::PDFoutput[]
image::media\SigilNameeBookFile_300dpi.png[]
endif::PDFoutput[]
+
. Close the Sigil app.

Congratulations, you made an ePub eBook.

=== Make Amazon Format eBook for Kindle
Although ePub is the most common ebook format, Amazon
decided to make their own format.
This means that Kindle readers can't read ePub without an
easy conversion to Mobi or Azw3 formats.

To get set up for this conversion, we'll load a free app
called Calibre.

.Free App Installation for Calibre
. Go to http://calibre-ebook.com.
. Select the **Download Calibre** button.
. Pick your operating system or OS.
. Select the **Download Calibre** link.
. After it downloads, install it on your computer.
+
NOTE: The Calibre manual is located at
https://manual.calibre-ebook.com.

.Conversion to Mobi using Calibre
. Open the Calibre app.
. Select **Add Books** and point Calibre to the folder
with your epub book file. Calibre imports the ebook and

lists your book as the top book on the list.
+
ifdef::HTMLoutput[]
.The ePub book loaded into Calibre
image::media\CalibreScreenShot1.png[]
endif::HTMLoutput[]

ifdef::PDFoutput[]
.The ePub book loaded into Calibre
image::media\CalibreScreenShot1_300dpi.png[]
endif::PDFoutput[]
+
. Select the book you want to convert to Mobi format for
Amazon reader devices.
. Select **Convert Books**. The convert window opens.
. If you want the Mobi format, select **mobi** as the
output format as shown.
+
ifdef::HTMLoutput[]
.Picking the Mobi Output Format
image::media\CalibreScreenShot2.png[]
endif::HTMLoutput[]

ifdef::PDFoutput[]
.Picking the Mobi Output Format
image::media\CalibreScreenShot2_300dpi.png[]
endif::PDFoutput[]
+
. If you want the newer Amazon AZW3 format, select
AZW3 as the output format as shown.
+
ifdef::HTMLoutput[]
.Picking the AZW3 Output Format
image::media\CalibreScreenShot3.png[]
endif::HTMLoutput[]

ifdef::PDFoutput[]
.Picking the AZW3 Output Format

```
image::media\CalibreScreenShot3_300dpi.png[]
endif::PDFoutput[]
+
. After Calibre shows the conversion job is done, select
the book in Calibre and select **Save to Disk**.
+
ifdef::HTMLoutput[]
.Saving the Converted Book
image::media\CalibreScreenShot1.png[]
endif::HTMLoutput[]

ifdef::PDFoutput[]
.Saving the Converted Book
image::media\CalibreScreenShot1_300dpi.png[]
endif::PDFoutput[]
+
. Find the *.mobi or *.azw3 format eBook on your computer
drive.
. Quit the Calibre app.
```

Another way to convert ePub to amazon format is to use
the free Amazon command line app called
KindleGen.footnote:[To download KindelGen, see URL
www.amazon.com/kindleformat/kindlegen]
At the time of publishing, Amazon even created a manual
for how to do it.footnote:[See Amazon's manual at URL
http://kindlegen.s3.amazonaws.com/AmazonKindlePublishingG
uidelines.pdf]

=== How to Test your eBook on Your Reader
We want to test our eBook before we send it out to the
world.
It's better when we catch mistakes before our audience
finds them.
We won't be perfect, but we want to seek as much
perfection as we can in our process for producing a book
for the world.

So how do we do this?

I offer a way.

You may find other ways you like better.

The point is be sure to test that your eBook works before you distribute it.

If you have a mobile device like a phone, you can load a reader app.

If you use the Android OS, load the Adobe Digital Editions app.

If you use iOS, then a reader app is pre-installed. It is called iBooks.

If you have no mobile device, but have a computer you can also load the Adobe Digital Editions app.

.One Way to Test a eBook

. Check that your device has an eReader app installed. If not, find one you like and install it. If you want one that works across platforms (Windows, MacOS, Linux) load the Adobe Digital Editions app.

. Make your eBook. Use the instructions in the rest of this book to make your eBook.

. Once you have your ePub file, in my example my file "Making_eBooks.epub" is the eBook version of this book.

. Get the eBook to your **iOS device**.

.. Email the *.epub file to yourself as an attachment.

.. Open the mail with your iOS device.

.. Click the *.epub attachment.

.. The iOS device will ask if you want to open it with iBooks. Select iBooks.

. Get the eBook to your **Android device**.

.. If your device has a removable SD or microSD card, copy the file onto that card and insert the card into the device.

.. Download and install FBReader on your Android device. You can get the FBReader reader app from Google Play.footnote:[See https://play.google.com/store/apps/details?id=org.geometerplus.zlibrary.ui.android]

.. On the Android device, open the FBreader app.

.. Select **File Tree | Memory Card** and navigate to the location of the *.epub file.

.. Select the book to view the metadata.

.. Select the **Read** button to open the book.

.. This is only one method. Use your favorite reader to check your book if you prefer. Other readers include Aldiko Book Reader, Adobe Digital Editions, and many other readers on Google Play.

. Get the eBook to your **Amazon Kindle device**.

.. Open your computer folder with the *.AZW3 or *.mobi file.

.. Plug your kindle into your computer with the USB charging cable. The Kindle device opens like another drive folder.

.. Drag and drop your *.AZW3 or *.mobi file from your computer folder to the Kindle folder.

.. Eject and disconnect your Kindle from the computer.

.. Remove the USB charging cable from the Kindle.

.. Open the Kindle and go to your library.

.. You should see your eBook listed as one of the books available.

. Review the eBook on the device eReader app.

.. Check that all your images came through the publishing process.

.. Check that the table of contents works.

.. Check that the cover shows up correctly.

.. Make sure your eBook is formatted so that it is readable.

TIP: Another way to get an eBook to your Reader and to your reviewer's readers is to put the eBook on Dropbox and send the URL to yourself and your reviewers. Once you go to the Dropbox URL, the rest of the steps are just like after the email is opened.

NOTE: I use the flowable eBook formatting meaning that the content flows onto the screen differently depending on the device screen size. For people used to fixed layout, there is a another format just for fixed layout but I don't care to mess with that layout. People that produce magazines may. If you really want to try for fixed layout on readers that can't even reliably produce tables yet, have at it. As for me, I am satisfied with the flowable eBook layout.

Colophon

This book used a set of tools that are all free and open source. The authoring was **plain text** using the free and open source text editor, **Atom** editor [20: https://atom.io/] in a plain text format called **AsciiDoc** [21: http://asciidoc.org], a text-based markup language similar to markdown but able to handle more complex documents. The asciidoctor-pdf app has not been corrected enough for footnotes to be at the bottom of the page. This is a failing. I may have to go back to DocBook processing to get the footnotes working for print. However, any text editor will do. For windows notepad++ is a great free tool too.

Version control was performed with the free and open source tool **git** [22: https://git-scm.com].

I prefer a modular content architecture rather than a single monolithic large document. I created the content in modular pieces (files) like legos. The main AsciiDoc file acts as a module map to the component files using the AsciiDoctor *include* statement.

Unfortunately for you, I am not a trained graphic artist and as an independent publisher, I have zero budget for hiring the artwork out. So you get what I make up or what I can find on sites with free usage rights and no licensing fees.

The media files get inserted by reference like with HTML and XML rather than embedded, making it easy to update them as needed with Gimp [23: https://www.gimp.org].

I used the AsciiDoc source content to make the HTML5 versions, PDF versions for print, and ePub [24: http://idpf.org/epub] versions for eBooks. For the HTML versions, I used an open source tool called Asciidoctor [25: http://asciidoctor.org] that runs on the Ruby command line. [26: http://www.ruby-lang.org. It does not require programming in Ruby, only installing Ruby.] A short command automatically converts the the plain text files into HTML.

For the epub version, I used Sigil [27: https://sigil-ebook.com] to create the ePub for the eBook. This was not quite automatic. However, other than importing (1) the HTML made from Asciidoctor, (2) the cover image, and (3) auto-generating the table of contents, making an eBook was easy with this tool. I recommend it. I've tried Pandoc [28: http://pandoc.org/] and Asciidoctor-epub, but both had issues that made the epub not pass the distributor's checks. This could have been my knowledge level at the time, too.

For reviewers wanting to use Microsoft Word, I auto-converted the HTML to Word. Reviewers made change annotations in Microsoft Word that were incorporated into the AsciiDoc source files with versioning using git.

Some reviewers prefer PDF to review. For PDF, I used Asciidoctor to convert the asciidoc file to DocBook XML [29: http://www.docbook.org] automatically and then used asciidoctor-fopub [30: https://github.com/asciidoctor/asciidoctor-fopub] to automatically generate the entire PDF. This process takes a few seconds once you complete the non-recurring setup tasks.

At first glance this tool set may sound complicated; however, I have found working with AsciiDoc far easier than working directly with HTML5 elements, XML, Word or Pages files.

The text files with AsciiDoc markup are easy for humans even if tools like Word and Pages keep changing and don't take this format 20 years later.

Glossary and Acronym List

This glossary and acronym list helps make clear the meaning of the words and acronyms used in this book. There are some terms where different people mean different things.

 I use lower case for glossary entries as a convention.

A

application (app)

Application software (also called end-user programs) include such things as word processors, Web browsers and spreadsheets.

ascii

Abbreviated from American Standard Code for Information Interchange, it is a character encoding standard. ASCII codes represent text in computers and other devices. The first computer character-encoding schemes were based on ASCII.

asciidoc

A format for plain text documents similar to markdown but that allows for complex documents. It leverages the DocBook XML standard.

author

The person or entity who created the content of the book. Most often the author writes the text. If more than one person is involved, the word contributor is often used, especially for graphics, cover art, etc..

C

colophon

A brief listing of production information.

D

DocBook

An XML DTD used for structuring book texts. The text of the book contains XML markup that divides it up into parts, chapters, paragraphs, tables, lists, footnotes and so on. The markup is structural and semantic, rather than having anything to do with how the text content should be presented, and the docbook can be processed automatically to create ebooks, large print, conventional print, synthetic audio versions of the book. [31: Definition from Harper Collins, at http://filestore.harpercollins.co.uk/prepress/mirrored_docs/glossary.html]

draft

The book's content at a particular point in time. Typically a first draft is followed by later drafts. The final draft is self-published.

E

eBook

An electronic version of a book that is read using mobile devices with reader apps or on a laptop or desktop if a reader app is installed. It is essentially a self-contained website in a zip file.

epub

EPUB is an e-book file format with the extension .epub that can be downloaded and read on devices like smartphones, tablets, computers, or reader apps. It is a free and open standard published by the International Digital Publishing Forum (IDPF). The term is short for electronic publication and is sometimes styled ePub. [32: https://en.wikipedia.org/wiki/EPUB]

F

footnote

A reference, citations or additional information that is not in the content flow, but is formatted at the end of ebooks and at the bottom of the page in print books. It typically uses a link to go from the footnote reference number to the footnote text. For print, the number still exists, but the finding of the footnote text is manual on the part of the audience.

H

HTML

Hypertext Markup Language.

I

index

An alphabetical list of specific key words in a book and the pages on which they are mentioned. This only applies to print books. eBooks presume full text search and don't typically include an index.

iteration

The repetition of a process.

L

layout

The design of a the pages. This book uses flowing layout that changes depending on the device screen size used. Even the print layout uses flowing content. Layout addresses the arrangement of text, images, titles, page numbers, and fonts used.

M

mindmap

A mind map is a diagram used to visually organize information. A mind map is hierarchical and shows relationships among pieces of the whole. It is often created around a single concept, drawn as an image in the center of a blank page, to which associated representations of ideas such as images, words and parts of words are added. Major ideas are connected directly to the central concept, and other ideas branch out from those. [33: Definition from Wikipedia at https://en.wikipedia.org/wiki/Mind_map.]

P

PDF

Portable Document Format. A file format that provides an electronic image of text and graphics that looks like a printed document and can be viewed, printed, and electronically transmitted.

print on demand (POD)

Publishing only when an order is received in small batches as small as one book.

prototyping

Prototyping for books is the activity of creating a table of contents or an incomplete version of the book being authored. Think of a prototype as a draft version of your book that allows you to explore your ideas and show the intention behind your content structure or the overall design concept to potential audience members before investing time and money in authoring content the audience may not value. It is much cheaper to change a book early in the authoring process than to make changes after you write the book. So, consider building prototypes early in the process. Prototyping allows you to gather feedback from potential audience members while you are still planning and designing your book's content.

R

reader

(1) The audience member reading the book. (2) A software application that lets people read eBooks on mobile devices and computers.

render

To make the book by manipulating the source content into the final output format, usually with a software application that automates the conversion process to speed it up.

S

self-publish

A method of book publishing that bypasses traditional

publisher organizations. The author has to perform the tasks that publishing houses do. Recent software apps make this much easier than it used to be. Services like Amazon, and distributor sites like Smashwords provide worldwide distribution and handling of sales transactions. The author is responsible for the marketing of the book. This book facilitates self-publishing.

SGML

Stanardized General Markup Language. A technical standard for complex mark-up. The predecessor of XML.

U

Unicode

A computer character set that expands Ascii to include most characters in all the world's languages.

X

XML

Extensible Markup Language (XML) is a markup language that defines a set of rules for encoding documents in a format that is both human-readable and machine-readable.

Thank You

Thank you for purchasing this book. Please write a review on the site you purchased it.